GUSTAV KLIMT

GVSTAV KLIMT

by Dr. Ilona Sármány-Parsons

CROWN PUBLISHERS, INC. - NEW YORK

Title page: Photograph of
Gustav Klimt, 1908
Oesterreichische Nationalbibliothek, Bildarchiv, Vienna

Collection published under the direction of:
Madeleine Ledivelec-Gloeckner

Library of Congress Cataloging in Publication Data

Sármány-Parsons, Ilona.
Gustav Klimt.

(Q.L.P. art series)
1. Klimt, Gustav, 1862-1918 — Criticism and
interpretation.   I. Title.
N6811.5.K55S27   1987   759.36   86-16050
ISBN 0-517-56178-6

Printed in Italy – Industrie Grafiche Cattaneo s.p.a., Bergamo
© 1987 Bonfini Press Corporation, Naefels, Switzerland

THE OLD BURGTHEATER, 1888-1889
Gouache on paper, 32¼″ × 36¼″ (82 × 92 cm).   Historisches Museum der Stadt Wien, Vienna

To Nicholas

*Whoever wants to know about me as a painter
— the only topic of any interest — should study
my pictures with care, and try to draw from
them what I am and what I am trying to do.*[1]

(1) Quoted from Christian M. Nebehay, ed. *Gustav Klimt- Eine Dokumentation*. Vienna: Galerie Ch.M. Nebehay, 1969, p. 40.

Very often do great artists hide behind their work. Klimt's remark suggests a reclusive character, withdrawn from the turmoil of public artistic life, who dedicated himself solely to his work. But there is a contradiction between the self-created image of the artist and the man himself. He was both fêted and reviled, adored and hated, and he became a dominant figure in Viennese art. He was one of the founders, and ultimately the leader, of the Secession movement. As a painter he was acutely conscious of his public role, and he fought fiercely to achieve his artistic goals.

How is this contradiction to be resolved? Klimt's contemporaries believed him to be genuinely self-effacing, even introverted. He could, however, be intransigently belligerent about his artistic ideals, and an uncompromising defender of his principles. His strength of character and single-mindedness were such that he succeeded in influencing the whole spectrum of the fine arts in turn-of-the-century Vienna. Notwithstanding the achievements of his contemporaries, his name is today virtually synonymous with the great burst of creativity that marked the dying days of the Austro-Hungarian Empire. As Hans Tietze wrote:

> His personality brought into focus both the merits and the flaws of Viennese painting.... He brought it out of the isolation in which it was atrophying and back into the mainstream of the world. Because of him Viennese painting became again aware of its own vitality and it established itself in a position that differed sharply from trends in German and other contemporary painting. More than anyone else it was Klimt who, at the turn of the century, guaranteed Vienna's individuality in art.[1]

Klimt's rise in the long turn of the century was due in part to a solid artistic education grounded in craftsmanship. He was born in 1862 to a lower-middle-class family of Moravian peasant stock. His father made a very modest living in Vienna as a goldsmith and engraver. His mother was Viennese born. Klimt and his two brothers were sent to the School of Arts and Crafts (Kunstgewerbeschule) to become good craftsmen capable of earning a living from their work. Because of his family's increasing hardship, the young Gustav Klimt was soon obliged to support them financially, and he continued to do so until he died.

The School of Arts and Crafts was a novel institution at the time. Founded on an English model, it offered a thorough artistic education of a very high standard. It provided technical skills as well as detailed instruction in the styles of earlier periods, reflecting the prevailing enthusiasm for historicism. Exceptionally gifted students were selected to attend Ferdinand Julius Laufberger's classes in decorative painting, thus receiving a schooling that was equal in quality to that of students of the Academy of Fine Arts.

(1) Hans Tietze. "Wiens heiliger Frühling war Klimts Werk," in *Kunstchronik*, XIX (1917-1918), 21, Leipzig.

ALLEGORY OF SCULPTURE, 1889
Pencil and watercolor heightened with gold on cardboard, 17¹⁄₁₆″ × 11¾″ (43.5 × 30 cm)
Oesterreichisches Museum für angewandte Kunst, Vienna

Drawing for the Poster for the First Exhibition
of the Vienna Secession, 1897
Pencil outline, India ink
corrections with white gouache
51³⁄₁₆″ × 31½″ (130 × 80 cm)
Historisches Museum der Stadt Wien, Vienna

Klimt's talent was quickly recognized at the School of Arts and Crafts, and by the age of twenty he was commissioned to do large decorative paintings. With his boyhood friend Franz Matsch and his younger brother Ernst Klimt, he had worked on designs for the Festzug, the great procession organized in 1879 to celebrate the silver wedding anniversary of the Emperor Franz Josef and Empress Elisabeth. The overall planning of this grandiose event was in the hands of the leading artist of the day, Hans Makart. He set the fashion for contemporary painting with his huge decorative canvases recalling the exuberance of Rubens and the golden tones of the Venetian School. He also initiated a style of interior design by turning his studio into a picturesque, elegant jumble stuffed with objets d'art from all ages. He largely determined the taste of the whole period, and when he died, in 1884, it was already clear that his mantle would fall on the up-and-coming Gustav Klimt.

After finishing their studies, the three close friends, Gustav and Ernst Klimt and Franz Matsch, decided to work together in the same studio. They jointly undertook the commissions that they received, mainly from an architectural firm, Fellner and Helmer, which specialized in building theaters. They became experts in this field, and during the 1880s they designed theater decorations all over the empire. Their work can be seen in Liberic, Karlovy Vary, and Rijeka. One of their most ambitious projects was the Romanian National Theater in Bucharest. Their fame grew with each commission. In 1885 they were given the important job of decorating, after designs by Makart, the Empress Elisabeth's favorite retreat, Villa Hermes near Vienna. For this project they executed large paintings illustrating scenes from Shakespeare's "A Midsummer Night's Dream."

The year 1886 marked a turning point. The studio was commissioned to decorate the staircase, ceilings, and lunettes of the new Burgtheater with scenes from the history of dramatic presentation. The Burgtheater was a national institution in Vienna, under the protection of

LOVE, 1895
Oil on canvas, 23⅝″ × 17⁵⁄₁₆″ (60 × 40 cm). Historisches Museum der Stadt Wien, Vienna

the Emperor. Its premieres were the greatest social and cultural events for both the aristocracy and the middle class. For the three artists this commission meant public recognition as officially established painters. Gustav Klimt chose themes from antiquity (*The Cart of Thespis, The Altars of Dionysos and Apollo, The Theater at Taormina*), together with a depiction of a performance of "Romeo and Juliet" at the Globe Theatre in Elizabethan times. His idea was to show the changing relationship between actors and their audience from earliest times. Historical accuracy, attention to detail in rendering materials and textures, and realistic psychological representation of character were the hallmark of these paintings. Klimt's style was then close to that of late Victorian history painters such as Lawrence Alma-Tadema and Frederic Leighton. In spite of the self-conscious nature of the composition, his paintings are a fresh and convincing celebration of the magic of the stage. They are also an early expression of a cult of the arts that in turn-of-the-century Vienna was partly aesthetic and partly spiritual.

The Burgtheater decorations were finished in 1888. They met with great public success, and the Emperor recognized the artists' achievement with the award of the Goldenes Verdienstkreuz. This was probably decisive in securing for Klimt a state commission that brought him to the height of fame: *The Auditorium of the Old Burgtheater*, a large gouache, which was painted in 1888-1889. It depicted all the contemporary personalities of the time—politicians, scientists, artists, and Viennese society beauties (see page 5). Klimt made over one thousand five hundred sketches for the painting. The most elevated and famous people in Vienna sat for him. The result was a technically astounding and original work, in which he depicted the members of the audience with nearly photographic faithfulness and yet preserved the spontaneity of the scene. He had successfully risen to the challenge of complete naturalism, although this type of naturalism was to be an artistic dead end. The enormous success of the picture and the widespread appreciation of its unique craftsmanship, its new approach to composition, and its naturalism were officially recognized with the award of the Emperor's Prize (Kaiserpreis) in 1890, consisting of four hundred gold gulden. The way was open for Klimt to become the most fashionable portraitist of his day and the presiding genius of the Academy of Fine Arts. It is a tribute to the strength of his creative drive and the depth of his artistic instincts that, at the peak of his popular success as a painter in the historicist mold, he turned away from the style that brought such rewards and toward Art Nouveau. Although at first glance he still appeared to be a historicist, the wall paintings for the staircase hall of the Museum of Art History already featured stylized forms and a new concept of female beauty that were early stirrings of the ideas of the Secession.

Klimt's style was not yet so radical as to offend traditionalists, and the studio's reputation for excellence ensured that the last great Ringstrasse commission was awarded to Klimt and his two associates. This was the decoration of the recently finished University Aula, for which appropriately allegorical and didactic paintings were required. The central theme was to be the victory of intellect over ignorance, and the four supporting panels were to illustrate the

Fishblood n.d.
Original destroyed
Pen and ink
From "Ver Sacrum" Nr. 3, 1898

Music, 1895
Oil on canvas, 14½″ × 17½″ (37 × 44.5 cm)
Bayerische Staatsgemäldesammlungen
Neue Pinakothek, Munich

12

four schools: Theology, Philosophy, Law, and Medicine. By the time of this commission the Matsch-Klimt studio was breaking up. Matsch was concentrating on flattering society portraiture, a business he cultivated through his acquaintances among the stars of the Burgtheater. Klimt's artistic interests were moving in another direction. It followed that they could no longer work in a homogeneous style. The area to be decorated was divided into distinct panels; Matsch took the central panel and one school allegory, and Klimt took the other three allegories. This division of labor signalled a break with the past, and it can be seen as Klimt's first step toward artistic independence.

THE YEARS OF CRISIS

By 1892 the thirty-year-old Gustav Klimt was an immensely popular painter. Had he so wished, he could have occupied a niche in the Viennese cultural establishment and looked forward to a long career as both a respected professor and prosperous Establishment painter. None of this happened, however, for a surprising transformation occurred in his career and his personality. We know little about the psychological roots of this metamorphosis, but it appears that his view of the world was radically altered. Klimt's personal life at this time is hard to document. His unwillingness to discuss either his feelings or his art was already legendary, but during this period family tragedies seem to have affected him deeply and made him even more taciturn. In 1892 his father died, followed shortly afterward by his brother Ernst. The latter had been the member of his family to whom he had been closest, emotionally and artistically. His death may have triggered the depression that became a recurrent feature in Klimt's life. Depression seems to have been a family trait that chronically affected his mother and one of his sisters. There was also a curious public setback around this time. In 1893 Klimt was appointed professor at the Academy of Fine Arts, but the Ministry of Culture inexplicably refused to confirm him in

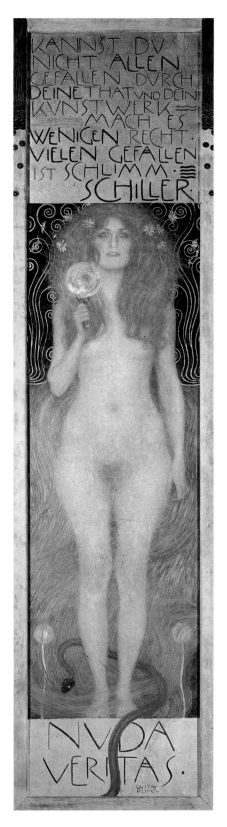

NUDA VERITAS, 1899
Oil on canvas
102⅜″ × 25⅜″ (260 × 64.5 cm)
Oesterreichische Nationalbibliothek
Theatersammlung, Vienna

◁
PORTRAIT OF SERENA LEDERER, 1899
Oil on canvas, 74″ × 33⅝″ (188 × 85.4 cm)
The Metropolitan Museum of Art, New York
Catharine Lorillard Wolfe Collection, Wolfe Fund,
Gift of Henry Walters, Bequest of Collis
P. Huntington, Munsey and Rogers Fund

SONJA KNIPS, 1898
Oil on canvas, 57⅛″ × 57⅛″ (145 × 145 cm)
Oesterreichische Galerie Vienna

15

PALLAS ATHENA, 1898
Oil on canvas, 29½″ × 29½″ (75 × 75 cm) without the frame
Historisches Museum der Stadt Wien, Vienna

the appointment, although he was obviously the most appropriate candidate. Such an injustice on the part of the Establishment is likely to radicalize any strong creative personality. This incident occured when Klimt was at the crossroads of academic realism and rebellious experiments, and it may have pushed him firmly in the direction of cultural opposition. He steeped himself in contemporary philosophy and literature with the passion of an autodidact who had not been able to avail himself of a university education. His solid artistic grounding in historicism had made him aware of the literary and philosophical content of art, and his cast of mind made his approach to art highly intellectual. He extended his amazing knowledge of the ornamental forms and styles of past ages to the newly discovered artistic heritage of forgotten cultures and Eastern civilizations, such as the Mycenaean and the Japanese. In the next five years he painted very little, only twenty-eight pictures in all, but each picture demonstrates the steady development of his personal style. He emerged from this period of crisis with an altogether new vision, and modern experiments were boldly featured in his paintings. As a result, those of his fellow artists who were looking for a reformation in artistic taste did not hesitate to accept him as their leader.

This was a time of ripening changes in Austrian culture. The crisis of liberalism and ever-growing social tensions in the Austro-Hungarian Empire were causing rapid and controversial transformations in literature and philosophy. Initially, Klimt perceived these changes mainly through literature. The modern literary renaissance that had gathered momentum in Germany was spreading to Vienna, and a circle formed around the influential critic Hermann Bahr. New voices gained a forum. Arthur Schnitzler published "Anatol" in 1892, and his "Liebelei" was first staged in 1895. Hugo von Hofmannsthal published his first poems in 1890, Rainer-Maria Rilke in 1894, and well-known Viennese feuilletonists published several small masterpieces of literary Impressionism. Klimt had personal contact with this very active intellectual circle, partly through his friendship with the painter Carl Moll and partly through the Flöge family. Emilie Flöge, the sister of his widowed sister-in-law, became his lifelong love. She epitomized the highly educated modern woman who could be an intellectual companion as well as a lover. From the mid-1890s on, Klimt became a force in the avant-garde and moved in the most refined circles of artists, and their patrons and admirers. He was exposed to many different influences, which he analyzed methodically in order to absorb only those elements that could benefit his artistic development; he rigorously avoided pastiche. Initially, he went beyond the images of antiquity typical of late historicism, which were sometimes rendered banal by an artist's insistence on a quest for archeological precision and a literal-minded approach to characterization. Klimt discovered the art of pre-classical Greece, especially the painted vases he could study at the Museum of Art History. Other influences included the Munich Secession, which found an audience in Vienna; the latest development in French painting, as revealed in the "Revue blanche"; and English artistic events reported in the "Studio." There were even a few Symbolists—James Whistler, Félicien Rops, Hans Thoma, and Max Klinger—on show in Vienna at the exhibition of the Gesellschaft für vervielfältigende Künste in 1895.

Tragedy, 1897.   Black chalk, pencil and gold, 16¾″ × 12⅛″ (41.9 × 30.8 cm)
From "Allegorien" Neue Folge, Nr. 66, 1897.   Gerlach und Schenk, Vienna

Junius, 1896.   Black chalk, pencil and gold, 16⅜″ × 12³⁄₁₆″ (41.5 × 31 cm)
From "Allegorien" Neue Folge, Nr. 53, 1895-1901.   Gerlach und Schenk, Vienna

Lady Sitting in an Armchair, n.d.
From "Ver Sacrum" Nr. 1, 1898

Untitled, 1899
Black chalk, 7" × 6⁷⁄₁₆" (18 × 17.5 cm)
From "Ver sacrum" Nr. 5, 1899

The French influence was the first to become evident in Klimt's work. His precisely executed and academically schooled drawings became lighter, the lines more sensitive, making the viewer aware of the living flesh. Classical models were replaced by a modern, unorthodox, yet sensual type of beauty. He painted half-length portraits of women using a hatching technique, in which the character is brought to life with delicate, barely noticeable mergings of black, gray, and white tones.

Love (see page 9) is a remarkable work of this period of transition. Made for the series of *Allegories and Emblems* commissioned by the art publisher Martin Gerlach, it looks as if it were an illustration to a story by Schnitzler. The lovers are painted with photographic clarity and are enveloped in a lilac-gray shading, as if standing in a garden at twilight. The tall, narrow field of the painting is framed by two golden borders adorned with pink roses. At first glance

SCHUBERT AT THE PIANO, 1899. Oil on canvas. Destroyed by fire in 1945. 59″ × 78⅝″ (150 × 200 cm)
Photo: Courtesy Galerie Welz, Salzburg

the scene is idyllic. On closer examination, baleful portents emerge in the composition. Only the young woman is absorbed in the dream of first love; her devotion is observed by her more experienced lover, whose expression verges on distrust. Far above them, as if from a nightmare, heads rise from the mist, symbolizing the different ages of woman. It is in this great early work that Klimt's preoccupation with love as something inseparable from death first comes to the fore. This theme was to become a leitmotiv of his whole œuvre in different guises and contexts (*Philosophy*, *Medicine*, the *Beethoven Frieze*, *The Kiss*, *Death and Life*).

The year 1895 saw the birth of another major work. The first version of *Music* (see page 12) was an early example of decorative Secessionist painting, composed as a flat, archaic frieze. Many Art Nouveau pictures were inspired by music, which played an important role in late-nineteenth-century aesthetic movements. Klimt's *Music* evokes the archetypal vocation of the art. The Greek priestess with a gold cithara is depicted as a tragic muse who can tame the cosmic powers of nature and man's bestial instincts, represented by the figures of Silenus and the Sphinx. In this canvas Klimt explored a second theme besides that of the duality of Eros and Thanatos: the cathartic and healing power of art, which he saw as the only force capable of vanquishing the destructive powers that man had unleashed. Carl Schorske observes that *Music* provides clear evidence that Klimt was already familiar with the philosophy of Schopenhauer and Nietzsche.[1] If Schorske is right, it would indicate that Klimt had studied the works of these philosophers in depth as a preparation for the great task of creating a modern representation of Philosophy and Medicine for the University Aula.

Sketch for "Medicine" 1900
Black chalk and pencil, 33⅞" × 24⅜" (86 × 62 cm)
Albertina, Vienna

By the end of 1896 the thirty-four-year-old Klimt had become boldly experimental; his graphic works were every bit as avant-garde as those of the French and Belgian masters of Art Nouveau. However, his strong attachment to classical mythological themes and traditional allegories remained. This reference to classic antiquity was typical of Viennese culture at the turn of the century,

(1) Carl E. Schorske. *Fin-de-siècle Vienna. Politics and Culture.* New York: Knopf, 1980, p. 221.

as evidenced by Hofmannsthal and Freud. It gave a special flavor and a sophisticated, scholarly hallmark to the coming years of the modernist movement.

IN THE VANGUARD OF SECESSION

The artistic unrest in Vienna finally came to a head in 1897, when those artists who had absorbed modern influences rebelled against the narrowly conservative clique controlling the Künstlerhaus, which held a monopoly on art exhibitions. Tired of the bigotry and suppression of talent practiced by the selection committee, forty members of the Künstlerhaus resigned in the spring of 1897 and founded a new association, the Secession (Vereinigung bildender Künstler Österreichs). They promptly elected Klimt as their president.

The aims of the Secessionists were not clearly defined. They wanted above all to be free of the tyranny of official taste that prevented

Study for "Medicine" c. 1901
Black chalk on paper, 15″ × 10¹⁵⁄₁₆″ (38.2 × 27.9 cm).
Albertina, Vienna

good modern work from being exhibited. They also wanted to ally themselves with the trends that were conquering other West-European countries. These rather general goals were given practical expression by two concrete developments — the publication of a journal, "Ver Sacrum," and the building of an exhibition hall. Like most revolutionaries, they seemed to want too much too soon — nothing less than a triumph over historicism in its own conservative stronghold of Vienna and, more importantly, a new approach to man in his environment, in which art was to play a vital role. They achieved recognition in only two years, and they brought about a radical change in public taste. The times were propitious for such a success, since people were beginning to chafe under the hegemony of a conservative academicism that had severely constricted the art market in comparison to Berlin or Munich. Moreover, an awareness was gaining ground that Vienna had become an artistic dead end, cut off from the progress evident elsewhere. Creative energies that were stifled urgently sought a forum, which the Secessionists were able to provide. At the same time, it was clear that Art Nouveau embodied a cult of art that found a genuine resonance in traditional Viennese culture. Ever since the golden age of the Baroque, the fine arts, architecture, and music had been part of social as

MEDICINE (final state), 1900-1907.
Oil on canvas. Destroyed by fire in 1945. 169⁵⁄₁₆″ × 118⅛″ (430 × 300 cm).
Photo: Courtesy Galerie Welz, Salzburg

HYGEIA, 1900-1907.   The only color photograph left to us from the three University paintings.
From "Das Werk Gustav Klimts"
Hugo Heller Kunstverlag, Leipzig, Vienna, 1918

PHILOSOPHY (final state), 1899-1907.
Oil on canvas. Destroyed by fire in 1945. 169⁹⁄₁₆″ × 118⅛″ (430 × 300 cm)
Photo: Courtesy Galerie Welz, Salzburg

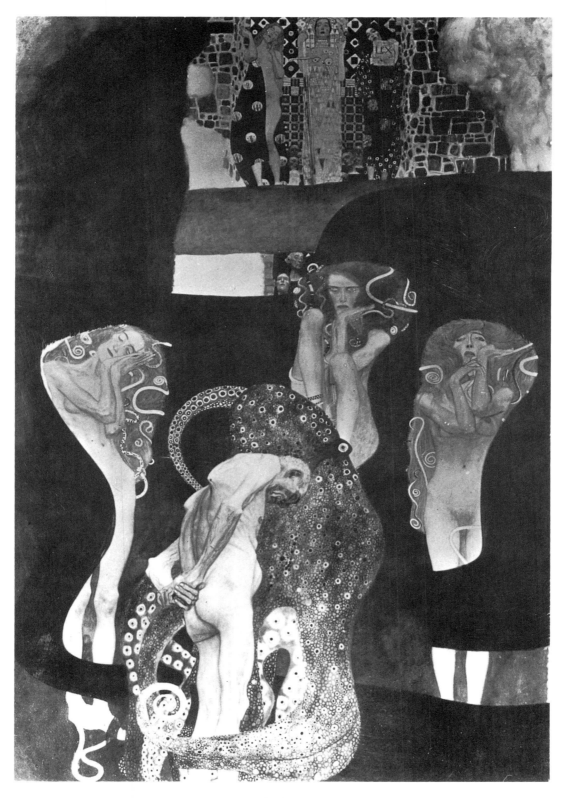

JURISPRUDENCE (final state), 1903-1907.
Oil on canvas. Destroyed by fire in 1945. 169⁵⁄₁₆″ × 118⅛″ (430 × 300 cm).
Photo: Courtesy Galerie Welz, Salzburg

FRUIT TREES, 1901
Oil on canvas, 35½″ × 35½″ (90 × 90 cm)
Private collection, New York

28

well as cultural values in Vienna. By the late nineteenth century, liberalism in all branches of art had found staunch patrons and the arts had acquired the greatest social prestige.[1] Now a new generation of artists was raising the cry for reform, breaking out of the artistic straitjacket of social, political, and aesthetic conservatism. They carried through their rebellion with such energy that victory was theirs almost immediately. This success in turn encouraged an even more ambitious—and ultimately illusory—project, that of changing society through the arts.

The Secessionists chose a symbolic title for their journal: "Ver Sacrum" (Sacred Spring). It was first published in 1898. Klimt was a member of the editorial committee for two years, and he contributed numerous prints and drawings. The first exhibition of the group was awaited with mounting excitement on the part of the public. It opened its doors in March 1898. Klimt had designed its poster, *Theseus Fighting the Minotaur* (see page 8). The poster stood for the victory of youth over barbarism with the help of goddess Pallas Athena, patron of wisdom and art. In the original version, Theseus was drawn without the traditional fig leaf, and this shocked the censor. Klimt was forced to substitute a more modest representation. In spite of this concession to propriety, the poster heralded a new graphic style with its unusual archaization, clearly inspired by Greek vase painting.

Many foreign artists were invited to the first exhibition, including Frank Brangwyn, Arnold Böcklin, Eugène Carrière, Alphonse Mucha, Pierre Puvis de Chavannes, Fernand Khnopff, Pavel Petrovitch Trubetskoy, Constantin Meunier, and Auguste Rodin, representing a wide range of artistic trends, from Naturalism through Symbolism and Art Nouveau to the masters of Realism. The show met with tremendous success. Even the aging Emperor visited the exhibition, where he was welcomed by the even more aged aquarellist Rudolf von Alt, who was honorary president of the Secession. The public flocked to see the show, and many pictures were sold. The original Secessionists who gathered around Klimt—Koloman Moser, Carl Moll, and Alfred Roller among them—found an influential ally in Otto Wagner, the professor of architecture at the academy. He began to experiment with new styles, and men like the architects Josef Olbrich and Josef Hoffmann followed his lead and became the creators of the Viennese version of Art Nouveau, known as "Secession style." The Secessionists' exhibition hall was designed by Olbrich, although its puritan geometric form owed a lot to the sketch supplied by Klimt. It is an extraordinary building, reminiscent of an Egyptian temple and crowned by a filigree globe of gilded laurel leaves. Over the entrance is the famous motto coined by the art critic Ludwig Hevesi: "To the Age Its Art, to Art Its Freedom" (Der Zeit ihre Kunst, der Kunst ihre Freiheit). This was the clarion call of the new generation, expressing a mixture of energy and idealism and a determination to sweep away all that had gone before. This avant-garde found loyal supporters and magnanimous patrons among leading Jewish families

(1) Carl E. Schorske. "Österreichs ästhetische Kultur 1870-1914," in the catalogue of the exhibition *Traum und Wirklichkeit*, Vienna, 1985, pp. 13-16.

Portrait of a Woman with Cape and Hat, n.d.
Black and red chalk, 17½″ × 12½″ (44.6 × 31.8 cm).   Albertina, Vienna

Head of a Young Girl. Study for a Performance of "Romeo and Juliet" at the Globe Theatre, n.d. Black chalk, stump, and white highlights, 10⅞" × 16¹¹⁄₁₈" (27.6 × 42.4 cm). Albertina, Vienna

in the Austrian upper middle class. The steel magnate Karl Wittgenstein, the textile magnate Fritz Wärndorfer, and the Knips and Lederer families supported the Secessionists wholeheartedly. Their farsightedness and instinctive reverence for art allowed Klimt and his circle to experiment.

Klimt's first great commission from this new group of patrons was the music room in Nikolaus Dumba's Ringstrasse mansion. Dumba was a rich businessman of Greek origin who had a reputation as a patron of the arts. Twenty-five years earlier he had asked Hans Makart to design his study. Now, in 1898, he employed the most fashionable artist of the day to create an entire music environment, complete with furniture, fittings, and two paintings over the entrance. One panel was the second version of *Music* (since destroyed by fire), more linear and decorative than its by now celebrated predecessor. The other was *Schubert at the Piano* (since destroyed), a warm impressionistic rendering of Vienna's most loved musical genius (see page 21). Carl Schorske notes:

> In these two panels Biedermeier cheerfulness and Dionysian inquietude confront each other across the room. The "Schubert" panel represents Hausmusik, music as the aesthetic crown of a social existence both ordered and secure. The whole is bathed in warm candlelight, which softens the outlines of the figures to blend them into social harmony.... Adapting impressionistic techniques to his service, Klimt substitutes nostalgic evocation for historical reconstruction. He paints us a lovely dream, glowing but insubstantial, of an innocent, comforting art that served a comfortable society.[1]

Contemporaries were enraptured by the painting. Although the picturesque "unfinished" style of Impressionism was unusual in Vienna at that time, the intimate poetical atmosphere of the scene, and the representation of Schubert, so dear to the hearts of the sentimental Viennese bourgeoisie, enchanted even the most conservative public. Hyperbole seemed hardly sufficient to do justice to its qualities. Hermann Bahr claimed that it was the most beautiful Viennese picture ever painted.

In 1898 another work was completed in the same flattering style, the portrait of *Sonja Knips* (see page 15). An earnest-looking woman with fine features sits on a garden chair against a background conventionally painted in dark brown tones. Her elegant dress of pink tulle floats about her. The dress seems to have a life of its own, and reminds the viewer of some rare and magical flower. This was the first portrait in which Klimt adopted a square canvas, which was to become his preferred format for paintings. It also featured another significant characteristic of Klimt's portraiture: The dress of the sitter plays just as important a role as the model herself. In a subtle manner, Klimt used the dress either to contrast with the character of the sitter or to stress some feature of her personality. In Sonja Knips's case it higlights the fresh youthful character of the sitter.

Lyrical impressionistic paintings with overtones of melancholy were only one facet of Klimt's output at the time. The second Secession exhibition displayed a more powerfully Dionysian side of his genius. His *Pallas Athena* (see page 16), though inspired by Franz Stuck's canvas, was markedly different from his two previous representations of the goddess. Instead of the calm, classically beautiful patron of wisdom and the arts, Klimt painted a dangerous red-haired femme fatale. Instead of Nikè, the winged victory, she holds in her hand *Nuda Veritas*, an unmistakably modern and sensual emblem of truth. Like Sigmund Freud, Klimt used figures from classical mythology to lay bare the deepest workings of the human psyche, especially the

(1) Carl E. Schorske. *Fin-de-siècle Vienna, Politics and Culture.* New York: Knopf, 1980, p. 220.

JUDITH AND HOLOPHERNE, 1901
Oil on canvas, 33⅛″ × 16½″ (84 × 42 cm)
Oesterreichische Galerie, Vienna

33

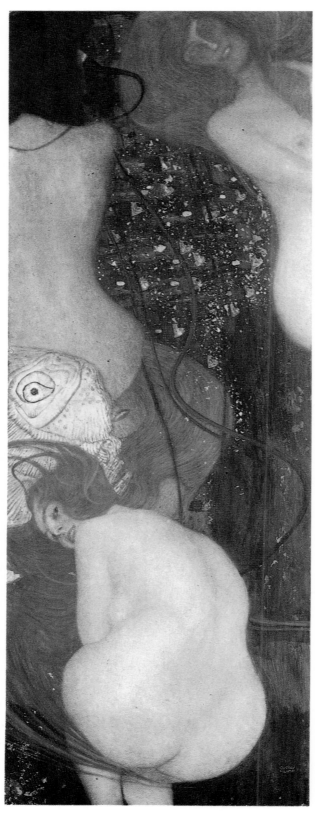

GOLDFISH, 1901-1902
Oil and gold on canvas, 71¼″ × 26¼″ (181 × 66.5 cm)
Schweizerisches Institut für Kunst
und Wissenschaft, Zurich

PORTRAIT OF EMILIE FLÖGE, 1902
Oil on canvas, 70 1/16" × 31 1/2" (178 × 80 cm)
Historisches Museum der Stadt
Wien, Vienna

BEECH GROVE I, 1902
Oil on canvas, 39⅜″ × 39⅜″ (100 × 100 cm)
Staatliche Kunstsammlungen, Gemäldegalerie Neue Meister
Dresden, East Germany

36

instinctual and erotic life. *Pallas Athena* achieves a fine balance between naturalistic detail and abstract ornamental form. It is at once erotic and detached, appealing and somewhat menacing. Not surprisingly, the public that was so enchanted with *Schubert at the Piano* received *Pallas Athena* with uneasiness and even hostility. This turned to dismay when it became clear that the "Demon of the Secession," as *Pallas Athena* was mockingly named, was merely the first example of Klimt's new naturalism. In his graphic work for "Ver Sacrum," Klimt elaborated on the disquieting figure of *Nuda Veritas*, which became a symbol of the threatening, instinctive female principle. The first version of *Nuda Veritas*, published in the first issue of "Ver Sacrum," typically belonged to Jugendstil Symbolism. It bore a characteristically high-flown quotation such as the early Secessionists delighted in: "Truth is a fire, and to speak the truth means to shine and burn."[1] Despite Klimt's self-confidence, the sensual, openly sexual quality of his work disconcerted the conventionally minded. They were confronted with a view of the world that subverted the existing order and openly questioned prevailing ethical assumptions and established values. The big oil *Nuda Veritas* seems at first glance to be simply the picture of a provocative red-haired nude. She is a creature of flesh and blood, without any of the idealization traditional in the paintings of nudes. The uninhibited naturalism of the work even dispensed with the taboo against depicting pubic hair, and this amounted to an open declaration of war against classical ideals (see page 13). The theme of the oil is that of art holding up a mirror to civilization, and it draws on a metaphor by Schopenhauer.[2] Most of the contemporary audience did not understand it. The work did not reveal its secrets easily, and perhaps was not intended to. It was Hermann Bahr who suggested the appropriate inscription for it, a quotation from Schiller to the effect that true art is only made by the few for the appreciation of the few.[3]

Before the storm of criticism burst over Klimt's head, he painted several lovely portraits. One of the finest is the 1899 portrait of *Serena Lederer* (see page 14), the wife of his patron Erich Lederer. Its composition and color show an indebtness to Whistler, but it is loftier and more ethereal than any of its precursors. The movement of the woman's long white robe makes the sitter seem taller and more imposing than she was in reality. The whole canvas is a graceful symphony in white, in the midst of which the viewer's attention is drawn to the soft black tresses and the large eyes full of warmth. The technique is close to that of Pointillism, with short, dense brushstrokes.

In 1899 new works seemed to be few and far between, because Klimt concentrated on the huge composition of *Philosophy*, which was to become a synthesis of his view of the world (Weltanschauung) and his experiments in style.

(1) *Wahrheit ist Feuer und Wahrheit reden heisst leuchten und brennen.* L. Schefer.
(2) Marian Bisanz-Prakken. "Programmatik und subjektive Aussage im Werk von Gustav Klimt," in R. Waissenberger, ed., *Wien 1870-1920, Traum und Wirklichkeit*, Salzburg: Galerie Welz, 1984, pp. 114-115.
(3) *Kannst Du nicht allen gefallen durch deine That und dein Kunstwerk, mach es wenigen recht. Vielen gefallen ist schlimm.* Friedrich Schiller, "Wahl," in *Votivtafeln*. See Karl Peltzer, *Das treffende Zitat*, Thun, Munich: Ott Verlag, 1957, p. 360.

... TO ART ITS FREEDOM

At the seventh Secession exhibition Klimt showed the uncompleted large oil painting of *Philosophy* destined for the University Aula. He wrote an explanatory note in the catalogue in order to clarify the picture's meaning:

> Left figure group: The Awakening to Life, Fertility, the Departure from Life.
> On the right: The Globe, the Mystery of the World, and a figure emerging from light, Knowledge.[1]

The painting sparked fierce debates in the press and elsewhere. Klimt had wrestled with this theme since 1894. Had he followed the traditional Baroque or classical model of allegorical paintings, he would not have aroused official opposition. However, in his quest for new insights, he sought not only to innovate through style but also to find a fresh approach to the theme's philosophical implications. His questioning mind had now begun to absorb the influence of Symbolism, and it embarked on an Odyssean voyage through the universe. He aimed at nothing less than unraveling in pictorial form the metaphysical puzzle of man's existence. His guides through this spiritual morass were Schopenhauer and Nietzsche. Klimt wanted to express the disorientation of modern man due to his having lost touch with the fundamental coordinates of his existence. The task he set himself was almost impossible: to depict in a painting the relationship of man and the universe. He sought to go further than conventional allegories allowed and to project the antirational philosophy of his time.

Klimt succeeded only insofar as it was possible to succeed in such an undertaking. The components of his iconography are somewhat traditional, but they are charged with a new interpretation. The fragment of the Wheel of Fortune in *Philosophy* is made from swirling living beings. The Sphinx, traditional custodian of the secret of life, occupies the center of the composition. On the left of the canvas, a stream of tangled bodies drifts into misty obscurity, next to the enigmatic sphinxlike spirit of the Universe, which is a barely recognizable and detached figure. In the lower foreground Knowledge emerges like a prologue. Her face is half-covered with a black veil, turned toward the viewer, but she offers only ambiguous assistance to those who would approach the secret of life (see page 26). The painting remained largely incomprehensible without a detailed exegis, which was provided by one of the Secession's most loyal supporters, the critic Ludwig Hevesi. His careful illumination of *Philosophy*'s themes was tacitly approved by Klimt. Perhaps it was a mixed blessing, for it made clear that the optimistic stance of philosophy, as it was taught at the university, was the very opposite of Klimt's vision. In *Philosophy* man is at the mercy of the universe and irrational, indifferent powers of nature. The river of life drifts in a haze of pain and suffering; from the beginning it is deeply imbued with death.[2]

(1) Official Catalogue of the seventh exhibition of the Secession, Vienna, 1900.
(2) Ludwig Hevesi. "Klimts 'Philosophie'," in *Acht Jahre Sezession*. Vienna: Carl Konegen, 1906, pp. 243-245.

Once the full import of the painting had been grasped, the university professors protested furiously this attack on orthodoxy: they had commissioned a painting on the theme of "The Triumph of Light over Darkness"; they were apparently presented with "The Triumph of Darkness over Everything." Klimt did not shrink from depicting proscribed themes such as disease, old age, physical decay, and poverty in all their painful ugliness. The Viennese preferred that art sugar the pill of reality, and they were shocked by this assault on their senses. However, twelve professors — among them Franz Wickhoff, the great art historian — defended Klimt's work. Wickhoff gave a provocative lecture at the Philosophical Society entitled "What Is Ugly?", in which he pointed to the historical relativity of the idea of beauty. Meanwhile, the professors hostile to Klimt tried to prevent the Ministry of Culture from accepting the picture for the university. A violent polemic filled the columns of the Viennese press. The ministry, however, adopted a policy of masterly inactivity. The picture's prestige was somewhat enhanced when it was awarded a gold medal at the Paris World Fair in 1900. Peace broke out, but only briefly, for in 1901 Klimt presented the next painting of the university commission, *Medicine.*

As in *Philosophy*, a large part of *Medicine* is occupied by a river of life, crammed with bodies swept along by the power of destiny (see page 24). From birth to death, all stages of existence are mingled, in various states of ecstasy and agony. All are the prey of illness and death. Hygeia, goddess of healing, turns her back on them (see also page 25). She faces the viewer in an hieratic stance. Stylistically, she is in stark contrast to the rest of the picture, stiff and decorative against a gentle flow of half-dreaming humanity. Enigmatic, she seems to proclaim the inter-dependence of life and death. Far from being the protagonist of enlightened science, she is the unmoved, ambiguous priestess of magic and of the occult power of healing. This pessimistic vision underlines the helplessness of medicine in the face of the unconquerable forces of fate, and it was understandably unacceptable to physicians. Like *Philosophy*, it undermines the positivist assumptions of a bourgeois view of the world and emphasizes the concept of nature as a great cycle fundamentally indifferent to the lone individual that is man. Both paintings were variations on Klimt's vision of the universe, a vision that was also Schopenhauer's:

> The World as Will, as blind energy in an endless round of meaningless parturience, love and death.[1]

The two pictures were also examples of Klimt's pluralism of style. The nocturnal cosmos of *Philosophy* resembles the star lights of Whistler's *Fireworks* pictures, the river of human bodies being soaked in a coolly mystical and bluish light. The realistic flesh and blood of *Medicine* are embedded in the warm glow of the pink and red tones of daybreak. In contrast, the gilded red robe of Hygeia creates ornamental stiffness as a tangible expression of the distance between the world of almighty gods and that of mortal man.

(1) Carl E. Schorske, *op. cit.*, p. 228.

The scandal of *Philosophy* had created an ideological issue; that of *Medicine* created also a political one. It alienated government officials who had previously supported Klimt. In Parliament, they defended the painting as much as they dared against attacks from both the Old and the New Right. However, the ministry refused to confirm Klimt's appointment when he was elected for a second time to a professorship at the Academy of Fine Arts.

Klimt's anger at this rebuff was partly expressed in his 1902 painting, *Goldfish* (see page 34). He had planned to call it *To my Critics*, until friends persuaded him to find a less aggressive title for this depiction of sensual women in provocative poses. Here was the uninhibited sexuality of the femmes fatales/water nymphs that was designed to shock public sensibilities. The public had already been disturbed by his *Judith* (see page 33), which lacked the polite, classical aura that usually surrounded a biblical figure. Judith is depicted as a lascivious Salome, a viciously menacing and decadent female, who combines appealing softness—conveyed in the warm flesh tones—with merciless cruelty. She emphasizes the duality of Eros and Thanatos, that recurrent theme of symbolist Secessionist art, which appears most vividly in Klimt's many paintings of beautiful but threatening women. The anger and bitterness suggested

Two Women Reclining, Embracing, n.d.
Red chalk, 14½″ × 22″ (36.8 × 56 cm). Landesmuseum Joanneum, Graz, Austria

WATERSNAKES, 1904-1907
Watercolor and gold on parchment, 19⅝″ × 7⅞″ (50 × 20 cm)
Oesterreichische Galerie, Vienna

THE BEETHOVEN FRIEZE, 1902
Mixed media: Casein, gold leaf, semiprecious stones,
mother-of-pearl, gypsum, charcoal and pencil on plates overall, 7′ 1″ × 98′ 12⅛″ (2 m 16 × 29 m 95)
Oesterreichische Galerie, Vienna

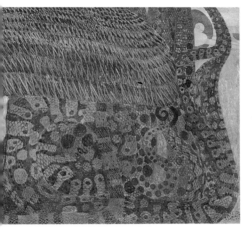

THE LONGING FOR
HAPPINESS
(detail)

THE HOSTILE
POWERS
(detail)

POETRY AND
GENIUSES
(detail)

THIS KISS FOR
THE WHOLE WORLD
(detail)

HOPE I, 1903
Oil on canvas, 74½″ × 26⅜″ (189.2 × 67 cm)
National Gallery of Canada, Ottawa

in *Goldfish* is more evident still in *Jurisprudence*, an allegory of law that turns conventional concepts of law and justice on their head (see page 27). Klimt's intention recalls Freud's apt quotation from Virgil's "Aeneid" at the head of "Interpretation of Dreams": "If I cannot bend the higher powers, I shall stir up hell" (Flectere si nequero superos, acheronta movebo). Instead of the humanistic world of law and justice, Klimt concentrates on the hell of punishment. A prisoner resigned to his fate stands at the center of the painting, a helpless victim of law. The hieratic goddesses of law float far above, luminous, and unattainable. The painting's symbolic idiom is rich in allusions to Greek mythology, which have been explored and interpreted within a psychoanalytical framework by American scholars of Klimt, such as Carl Schorske and Alessandra Comini.[1] Although Klimt never offered an interpretation of his own work, he clearly was familiar with the ancient Orestean myth. *Jurisprudence* alludes to the most archaic and brutal version of crime and its punishment, and it is a savage indictment of the Establishment's complacency with regard to its legal system. Instead of the usual allegories of Truth, Justice, and Law, the three serpent-flanked Eumenides—Tisiphone, Alecto, and Megaera—dominate the scene of an execution chamber, where an aged anonymous victim is about to be enfolded by a giant octopus. The octopus is Klimt's stark reinterpretation of an ancient idiom merged into a modern vision of punishment. In Mycenaean vase painting the octopus was merely a popular decorative motif. In *Jurisprudence* it becomes a symbol for harsh legal retribution. Later interpretations have sought to extend its range of metaphor to castration—the ultimate punishment for a symbolical Orestean crime.[2] This would place more symbolism on the image than it can bear, but Klimt clearly enjoyed shocking the prudish among the critics and the public when he painted extravagantly sexual archetypes.

The university canvases were stunningly new in both content and style. Klimt broke with traditional treatments of space, so that his figures float in an undefined perspective and the balance of the composition is controlled by the decorative relationship between color and form. Colors are symbolically significant, used to evoke mood and feeling. Hevesi compared the deep blue of *Philosophy*, with its sparkling stars, to a brightly polished slab of lapis lazuli. In *Medicine* everything is wrapped in a gradation of warm red tones, except for the figure of Death, whose blue veil is woven into the stream of human life. In *Jurisprudence* imaginary space is absorbed in a thick texture of deep black material, like a suffocating mass of hair, in which the furies are embraced by gold serpents. Klimt continued to work on the three large oils after they were exhibited. He elaborated on their details and colors until 1907. By 1905 it was clear that they would never be installed at the University Aula. He then sought the help of friends and patrons to force the Ministry of Culture to sell the paintings back to him. He poured out his heart in an interview with Bertha Zuckerkandl, a sympathetic art critic and journalist:

(1) Carl E. Schorske, *ibid.*, pp. 208-278.
    Alessandra Comini. *Gustav Klimt*. London: Thames & Hudson, 1975, pp. 24-25.
(2) Carl E. Schorske, *op. cit.*, p. 252.

PORTRAIT OF
HERMINE GALLIA, 1904
Oil on canvas
67⅛″ × 38″
(170.5 × 96.5 cm)
The National Gallery
London

PORTRAIT
OF MARGARETHE
STONBOROUGH-WITTGENSTEIN,
1905. Oil on canvas
70¹³⁄₁₆″ × 74¾″
(180 × 190 cm)
Bayerische Staatsgemälde
sammlungen, Neue
Pinakothek, Munich

Enough of censorship. I am having recourse to self-help. I want to get out. I want to get away from all these sterile absurdities that hinder my work, and get back to a state of freedom. I refuse all state patronage. I renounce everything.[1]

In other words, Klimt was determined to remain faithful to the Secession's motto, "To Art Its Freedom," even at the price of losing any prospect of future state commissions.

After Klimt's death the university paintings were acquired for the private collection of Erich Lederer. It is an unquantifiable loss to Austrian culture that these masterpieces of Viennese Symbolism were accidentally burned in 1945, together with many other paintings by Klimt, in a country house near Vienna where they had been placed for safekeeping during the war.

THE PYRRHIC VICTORY OF AESTHETICISM

In 1901, amid the violent controversy surrounding *Medicine*, Klimt was at work on an ambitious mural to accompany a statue of Beethoven by Max Klinger. The Secessionists had decided to make Klinger's work the focal point of an exhibition dedicated to the unification of all the arts (Gesamtkunstwerk). Klimt's *Beethoven Frieze* was to be a vital component of this major artistic event (see pages 42, 43).

For nearly a decade Klimt had been searching for an answer to questions about the purpose of man's existence. His work on the University Aula commissions convinced him that neither philosophy, nor medicine, nor least of all law held the key to man's happiness. Only the beautiful utopia of Secessionist Symbolism seemed to promise a solution. Only through art could man fully realize his potential for joyful existence.

The Beethoven exhibition was a turning point not only in Klimt's career, but also in the general attitude toward the arts in Vienna. An all-embracing concept of the role of art had begun to emerge, epitomized by the Gesamtkunstwerk, in which all the arts were pressed into service for the same idea. In the eyes of a committed new generation, art moved to center stage and took up a crucial task: nothing less than the regeneration of the world. Klimt and his circle regarded Beethoven as the incarnation of a genius that brings salvation to mankind through love and self-sacrifice. The Klinger statue was to be the apotheosis of a genius not bounded

(1) Bertha Zuckerkandl-Szeps. "Eine Scheidung soll es sein," in *Neues Wiener Journal*, Vienna, 2.5.1931. Reprint in O. Breicha, ed., *Gustav Klimt-Die Goldene Pforte*, Salzburg: Galerie Welz, 1978.

THE THREE AGES OF WOMAN, 1905
Oil on canvas, 70¹³⁄₁₆″ × 70¹³⁄₁₆″ (180 × 180 cm)
Galleria Nazionale d'Arte Moderna, Roma

Study for Adele Bloch-Bauer I, 1907
Black chalk, 17½" × 12⅛" (45.8 × 31 cm)
Albertina, Vienna

by time. Formally it recalled the legendary statue of Zeus by Phidias; it also referred to Prometheus and the Christian concept of salvation. All the other works in the exhibition were subordinate to this statue, and they were to elaborate on its mighty theme.[1]

Klimt chose to express the ideas of Beethoven's Ninth Symphony in a frieze following Richard Wagner's essay "Beethoven." The theme was simple: mankind longs for happiness; the hero chosen by the gods fights for man's salvation against evil. Some evil powers inhabit the inner life of man, such as lust, intemperance, and fear. Others are simply visited on him, such as disease, poverty, and death. The question of how the hero triumphs over these powers is left unresolved. He finds temporary respite from strife through poetry and then moves into a world of pure joy and love. There he finds his true companion, and the couple unite symbolically with the world in a healing kiss. The frieze, however, was overburdened with allegorical images of pagan and Christian origin, which Klimt interpreted in a highly personal way in an attempt to create a universally valid synthesis. He used stylization and archaism to create an appropriate framework for a daring abstract concept, but the intellectual complexity of the themes resisted visual representation. Art clearly needed to be more than the assertion of an idea to play a role in the salvation of modern man; theory was no substitute for

(1) The thorough reconstruction of the concept of this exhibition and of its iconographical program was made by Marian Bisanz-Prakken (*Der Beethovenfries*. Salzburg: Residenz Verlag, 1977).

50

emotional persuasiveness and immediacy. Despite the sophistication of Klimt's technique, the unusual, two-dimensional style of the frieze, the ugly models, and the consciously deformed figures struck the public as bloodless and wooden. The work was badly received and the exhibition something of a fiasco. It was intended as an apotheosis of the arts and the artist as a prophetic genius; it demonstrated only the weakness of Pan-Aestheticism. The hint of scandal attracted large crowds to the exhibition, but it proved to be a financial failure. This caused Klimt's group of extreme idealists to quarrel with the other members of the Secession movement, which was beginning to fragment and lose direction.

Klimt was out of favor with the public and, after the scandal of the university paintings, with the authorities as well. He was never again to receive a state commission. Even within the Secession, the confidence of his fellow artists was severely shaken by the controversies over the Beethoven frieze. However the 1903 retrospective show of his works was sufficiently impressive to still most of the critical voices temporarily, but ultimately the differences between the critics and Klimt's group were to prove irreconcilable. In 1905 Klimt and his friends, among them Carl Moll, Josef Hoffmann, Koloman Moser, and Otto Wagner, broke away, and the so-called Impressionists remained alone in the Secession.

After the university crisis Klimt turned to different themes for a while. In a 1903 solo show, he exhibited bewildering new pictures, in particular fine landscapes. He had begun painting landscapes relatively late in his career, during a summer holiday on Lake Attersee in 1898, where he stayed as a guest of the Flöge family. The early landscapes belong to the category of Central European genre known as "mood landscape" (Stimmungslandschaft), which was immensely popular among artists in that part of the world. They drew inspiration not from French Impressionists such as Claude Monet, but from such painters as James Whistler, who was regarded as the finest creator of mood and atmosphere, and the Belgian Symbolist Fernand Khnopff. Klimt's early landscapes bear witness to their influence and suggest inner silence and meditation in a natural setting. The power of these pictures lies in a mood created by a scene, and such a mood is to bring the essence of nature closer to the grasp of man. Human figures do not appear; the horizon tends to be set very high in the composition, the theme is nature itself and its abundant vegetation. By 1903 Klimt's vision of nature had been brought into harmony with his general vision of the world, and his pictures document a perception of nature as an organically coherent infinity. Ever since *Pallas Athena* Klimt had favored the square shape, and from 1899 onward his landscapes were painted on a square canvas. This was not an arbitrary choice. Klimt thought that the square shape creates an aura of calm around the subject matter and the square painting becomes then a segment cut out from a universal whole; the most striking characteristic of the square shape was that it could be extended in any direction like the pattern in a fabric. It is a fragmentary vision of a homogeneous world, a small rendering of something greater that has a mystic power. The sheer spectacle of nature did not interest Klimt as it did the French Impressionists, but rather its hidden essence, more

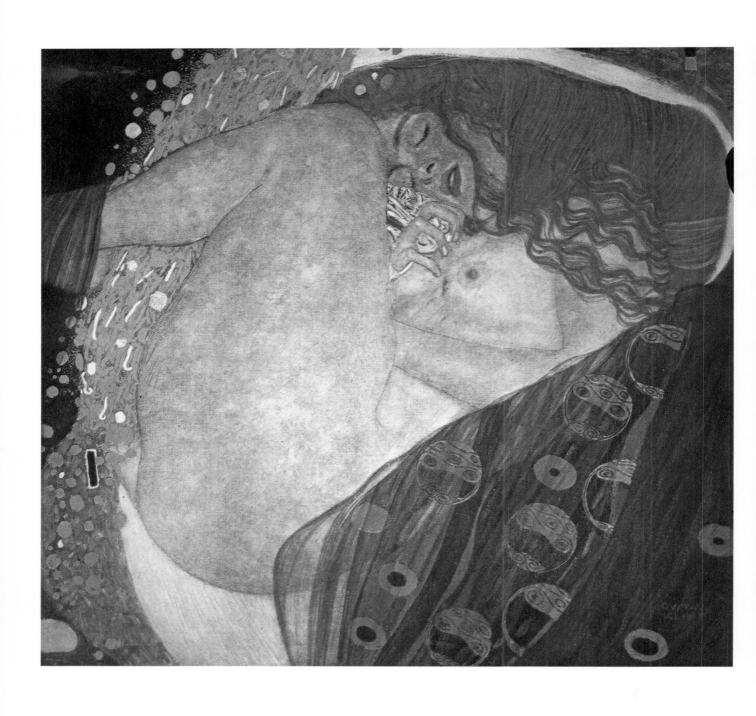

DANAE, 1907-1908
Oil on canvas, 30⁵⁄₁₆″ × 32⁵⁄₈″ (77 × 83 cm)
Galerie Würthle, Vienna

52

PORTRAIT OF ADELE BLOCH-BAUER I, 1907
Oil on canvas, 54⅜″ × 54⅜″ (138 × 138 cm)
Oesterreichische Galerie, Vienna

PORTRAIT OF FRITZA RIEDLER, 1906
Oil on canvas, 60³⁄₁₆″ × 52³⁄₈″ (153 × 133 cm). Oesterreichische Galerie, Vienna

COUNTRY GARDEN WITH SUNFLOWERS, 1905-1906
Oil on canvas, 43⅜″ × 43⅜″ (110 × 110 cm)
Oesterreichische Galerie, Vienna

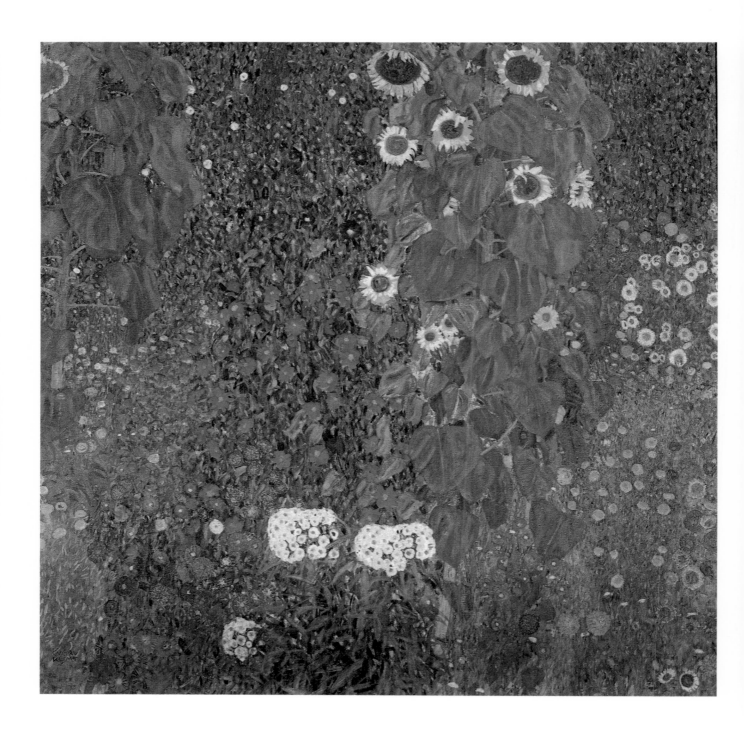

SUNFLOWER, 1905
Oil on canvas
(here in black and white)
43⅜″ × 43⅜″
(110 × 110 cm)
Private collection

precisely the principle of a natural continuum as a vital element, as can be seen from woodscapes that were painted during the period of the university controversy. Deep in a wood, a curtainlike dense pattern of parallel tree trunks marks a rhythm that could continue indefinitely. The trees and the foliage are painted in such a way as to create a sense of infinite texture (see page 36).

The portrait of his "eternal love," *Emilie Flöge*, was the other sensation of Klimt's 1903 exhibition. This was to be the first of many portraits of a woman placed in a bare environment, robed in elaborate ornamentation heightened with gold. She is posed like a mannequin in bizarre fancy dress. (This was not a whimsical depiction, for Emilie Flöge owned a successful boutique.) Only her face and hands are painted realistically. The slender figure becomes an exotic blue and purple flower, whose stem is overlayed with glittering symbolic ornaments see page 35). According to Alessandra Comini:

The interpretation of the shapes depends on almost oversimplified visual equation with traditional male and female symbols.... Klimt painted pollen and pistils, spermatozoa and ova interpenetrating both humans and nature.[1]

However, the eroticism of Klimt's ornamentation has a powerful aesthetic quality of its own and can be enjoyed regardless of whether the viewer is aware of their latent meaning or not. As he was often to do later, Klimt painted the decorative part of the picture with the precision of a goldsmith, thus turning the canvas into a masterpiece of art and craft. At this time he was creating many designs for Hoffmann and the artists of the Wiener Werkstätte — the crafts workshop of the Secession. He was also designing fashion textiles for Emilie Flöge's boutique. Within these rather narrow circles of the social and intellectual elite he could, therefore, realize his dream of an art that permeated man's environment.

Klimt's vigorous and strongly characterized drawings were also shown at the 1903 exhibition; the most striking were the sketches made for the *Beethoven Frieze* and *Jurisprudence*. Other drawings displayed a radically changed graphic style using new materials; for these he abandoned the rough-textured surfaces that he had favored earlier and adopted a finely made Japan paper, on which he simply drew in pencil, sometimes adding highlights in red, blue, or white. His marvelous female half-figure and an early version of the couple were drawn in this new style.

By 1903 Klimt and his associates were badly in need of generous patrons with open minds. The brief honeymoon that the vanguard of the Secession had enjoyed with the public was over for good. Most of the potential audience for art was unable to follow such increasingly complex experiments. Only a few connoisseurs appreciated the enigmas of Klimt's work. These were among the highest level of the rich bourgeoisie, and they continued to commission portraits of their wives and daughters. Klimt thus became a sort of court painter to the plutocracy, and the perceptive recorder of rich and high-strung ladies. These portaits betray the lingering influence of Whistler, such as in the picture of *Hermine Gallia* (see page 46). She poses in a frilled white dress, and patches of pink, blue, and green sparkle in the folds of her garment. She seems poised like a pirouetting white peacock. The young *Margaret Stonborough-Wittgenstein*, sister of the philosopher, is even more ethereal (see page 47). Standing before a wall studded with curious ornaments, she gazes wide-eyed at something beyond the viewer's sight. Her delicate features crown a slender figure draped in a weightless dress of fine white lace. Like so many of Klimt's portraits, the picture is pervaded by an atmosphere of melancholy, whose source cannot be defined. Klimt was such a perfectionist that hundreds of sketches went into the preparation of this and other portraits. Indeed, he persevered in his quest for exactly the effects he wanted long after the sitters considered the work finished to their satisfaction.

(1) Alessandra Comini, *op. cit.*, p. 14.

THE KISS, 1907-1908
Oil on canvas, 70¹³⁄₁₆″ × 70¹³⁄₁₆″ (180 × 180 cm). Oesterreichische Galerie, Vienna

INTO SECLUSION—THE GOLDEN STYLE

The year of his retrospective, 1903, was a milestone in Klimt's art. He visited Italy twice and was captivated by the golden mosaics of Ravenna. Although he had used gold on previous occasions, such as in *Pallas Athena*, *Judith*, *Goldfish*, and the *Beethoven Frieze*, it was after his trip to Italy that he entered his so-called golden period, which reached its peak in 1907.

During the course of Klimt's career, gold took on different symbolic meanings. In his earlier paintings it was used to emphasize sacred objects—the cithara in the hand of the priestess of Apollo, the helmet and armor of Pallas Athena. Subsequently, gold was associated with the sexual appeal of femmes fatales, as in *Judith*, *Goldfish*, and *Jurisprudence*, and it heightened the sensual suggestiveness of the patterns that adorned the women's robes. Even at the peak of his golden style, only those pictures dealing with general themes concerning mankind were dominated by gold. They belonged to an existing tradition of allegories, the Lebensrätsel, or "life enigma" works. These pictures became a medium for Klimt's meditation, elaborating on the allegories of man that first appeared in the river of human bodies in *Philosophy* and *Medicine*. Alice Strobl has recently remarked on how procreation, pregnancy, and birth are integrated into these allegories, as are disease, the terrors of old age, and death.[1] The flow of life itself became the dominant theme of Klimt's work.

"Ver sacrum" ceased publication in 1903. At the same time that he withdrew from the public arena, Klimt gave up the vague social content that his work had exhibited previously. He showed less and less sensitivity to social problems, and he retreated instead into an ivory tower of art. He seemed to have become embittered and to be indifferent to sociopolitical events. It is likely that at this time he turned to occult philosophy and Eastern religion, and he began to develop a view of the world in which only the eternal questions of life played a significant role. Dramatic events of the time were not reflected in Klimt's paintings. As the hermit lives intensely in his religious ecstasy, so Klimt became lost in another world of pure aestheticism. Increasingly, he concentrated on the biological nature and destiny of man, and those elements of existence that are valid for all individuals. Klimt still drew an income from portrait commissions, but for himself he took on the challenge of the Lebensrätsel, which stimulated him to ever greater efforts, regardless of whether the public would follow him into uncharted waters. The philosophical references of these compositions became increasingly enigmatic; yet their brilliant surfaces were so personal in style and so daringly modern in their approach that these qualities were to obscure the paintings' profound philosophical intent. On the surface, Klimt's art was now concerned with the private and the particular, such simple subjects as flowers and women. He celebrated women with bright colors and the resplendence of gems and gold. Although such representation of flowers and women gratified the sensual side of

(1) Alice Strobl. *Die Lebensrätsel in Gustav Klimts Werk*. Lecture held in May 1981. *Gustav Klimt, die Zeichnungen*, vol. I-III. Salzburg: Galerie Welz, 1980-1984.

HOPE II, 1907-1908
Oil and gold on canvas, 43½″ × 43½″ (110.5 × 110.5 cm)
The Museum of Modern Art, New York
Mr. and Mrs. Ronald S. Lauder and Helen Acheson, and Serge Sabarsky

his nature and was enjoyed for its own sake, his underlying goal was to capture the passing moment of sensual joy, the rapture of life. Eros and Thanatos became again a source of inspiration, but in a new guise.

Immediately following the completion of the embracing couple of the *Beethoven Frieze*, Klimt made a series of five drawings representing a couple in profile—a man with his arm around the shoulder of a pregnant woman. Pictures of pregnant women were generally regarded as unacceptable, and the representation of such a theme in *Medecine* had been one of the major reasons for the work's rejection. In the first version of *Hope* a young pregnant woman stands alone in a field carpeted with flowers. In the final overpainted version of the painting, the background teems with allegorical monsters, evil powers threatening the new life (see page 44). Next to the woman, whose stark naturalism shocked Klimt's contemporaries, are Vice, Illness, Poverty and Death. Many regarded the pregnant nude as obscene, although the treatment of the theme is anything but lascivious. For a long time the painting was tucked away in the private Wärndorfer collection, and even there it was hidden from view behind its altarlike shutters, which emphasized the sacred nature of the image. It was not shown to the public until 1909.

The transience of youth and beauty was the theme of *The Three Ages* (see page 49). After the *Beethoven Frieze* Klimt rarely painted men, and when he did it was always in relationship to women. Instead of vigorous male heroes, passive women occupy the center stage, their fragile forms obviously the prey of mortality as in *The Three Ages*. In these allegories of mankind, as Werner Hofmann calls them,[1] death is ever present—sometimes in the form of a skeleton or skull, sometimes as a swirling blue veil, which was Klimt's symbol of death since *Medicine*.

In the same year 1905 Klimt produced some of his most beautiful garden pictures. *Country Garden* (National Gallery, Prague) and *Country Garden with Sunflowers* (see page 56) were celebrations of abundant Nature. Like the earlier woodscapes, these works were painted on a square canvas, but, unlike them, the accent was on the dense texture of different sorts of plants such as groups of roses and clumps of sunflowers. Vincent Van Gogh had made the sunflower immensely popular with painters, who were attracted by its potential for anthropomorphic symbolism. Klimt's *Sunflower* was no exception (see page 57) and Ludwig Hevesi went so far as to write whimsically:

> [The sunflower] stands in resigned solitude among the other flowers as if it were a fairy in love.[2]

(1) Werner Hofmann. *Gustav Klimt und die Wiener Jahrhundertwende.* Salzburg: Galerie Welz, 1970.
(2) Ludwig Hevesi. "Weiteres über Klimt," in *Altkunst-Neukunst.* Vienna: Carl Konegen, 1909, p. 319.

POPPY FIELD, 1907
Oil on canvas, 43⅜″ × 43⅜″ (110 × 110 cm)
Oesterreichische Galerie, Vienna

WATER CASTLE, 1908
Oil on canvas, 43⅜″ × 43⅜″ (110 × 110 cm)
Narodni Galerie, Prague

At first glance the garden pictures seem to be Pointillist—*The Poppy Field* (see page 63) in particular appears to imitate late French Impressionism—but on closer examination these works go far beyond Impressionism. Johannes Dobai has shown that an "overlapping effect" creates an illusion of space while the surface retains the flatness of a textile design. The result is a synthesis between decorative effects and a cosmic sense of life suggested by a fragment of infinity.[1] This was the period when Klimt's decorative symbolism was most impressive. The sensuous appeal to the eye disguised a deeper and fully planned personal iconography. The cube, spiral, circle, and triangle, the colored foliage and golden arabesques recalled archetypal symbols of old religions. They enriched the paintings with their traditional allegorical references or with erotic associations.

Klimt's paintings operate on more than one level, as may be seen in the portraits of *Fritza Riedler* or *Adele Bloch-Bauer* (see pages 55, 53). Only the faces and the hands of the models are represented in three-dimensional reality. The space surrounding them is absorbed by the modulation of fantastic ornaments and color fields that flatten the painted surface and dissolve solid masses so as to create an ambiguous relationship between forms. The curious wall decoration behind Fritza Riedler suggests a headdress or wig reminiscent of those worn by the Spanish infantas in Velázquez's portraits. In the *Portrait of Adele Bloch-Bauer* similar decorative motifs overloaded with erotic symbolism are arranged in different sizes and rhythmic patterns, and they contribute swirling and pulsating effects to the otherwise geometric composition and the hieratic pose of the sitter. This technique introduces an element of eroticism and calls to mind Freudian analyses or the heroines of Robert Musil's novels. With their wide-open eyes and their sensitive hands, the women are clearly the restless, frustrated prisoners of their status and wealth, like richly plumed birds in gilded cages.

From 1905 to 1909 Klimt worked on the *Stoclet Frieze*, his last great mural. It consists of three marble mosaics inlaid with gold, enamel, and semiprecious stones. The commission came from Alphonse Stoclet, a Belgian steel magnate, and his wife, Suzanne, who had asked Josef Hoffmann and the Wiener Werkstätte to build their mansion in Brussels. This building was to become the masterpiece of Vienna Secessionist arts and crafts, and Klimt's task was to decorate the walls of the dining room. The Stoclets were enthusiastic collectors of Eastern art and owned many rare pieces of Indian and Buddhist sacred art. Their interest stimulated Klimt to further study Eastern art as he created designs for the mosaics. The finished work marked a high point in his assimilation of the form and content of Oriental art. On two long walls facing each other he designed two stylized Trees of Life, whose branches end in golden spirals. A young girl representing Expectation (see also page 54) dances under one tree. A couple embrace under the other, representing the idea of Fulfillment. The two trees may stand for the Tree of Life and the Tree of Knowledge in the Garden of Eden. Alice Strobl interprets

(1) Johannes Dobai. "Die Landschaft in der Sicht von Gustav Mahler. Ein Essay," in *Klimt Studien*, Salzburg: Galerie Welz, 1978, p. 260.

*Torso of a Young Girl
in Three-Quarter Profile, n.d.
Pencil drawing
Eidgenössische Technische Hochschule, Zurich
Graphische Sammlung*

the three birds of prey in the scene as symbols of death, so that the whole picture may be taken to represent the cycle of life.[1] A strong Eastern influence is also evident in the ritual pose of the dancer and the mystic emblem on one of the narrow dining room walls, probably a mandala, the Buddhist aid to meditation that stands for the universe.

The embracing couple under the Tree of Knowledge is one of Klimt's leitmotivs. Time and again he returned to this image to express the possibility of man's happiness. Sometimes it referred to personal happiness, while in the *Beethoven Frieze* it became a symbol of joy in life. In the *Stoclet Frieze* the embrace is once again intimate, even playful. Its most complete and powerful version was to be the famous painting known as *The Kiss* (see page 59), which may be seen as the crowning glory of Klimt's golden style, the masterpiece he presented at the 1908 Kunstschau in Vienna, which was the swan song of Viennese aestheticism.

After some years' absence from public view, Klimt's works reappeared in this comprehensive exhibition organized to celebrate the sixtieth anniversary of Franz Josef's ascent to the throne. Klimt was invited by the municipal authorities to plan the exhibition and to make the opening address. This turned out to be a summary of his artistic credo:

> No areas of human experience are too insignificant or humble to offer scope for artistic endeavor.... The progress of culture is based only on continual and progressive impregnation of life as a whole with artistic goals.[2]

(1) Alice Strobl. *Gustav Klimt, die Zeichnungen.* Salzburg: Galerie Welz, 1980-1984, vol. III, p. 91.
(2) *Katalog der Kunstschau 1908*, Vienna, 1908.

In 1908 his aestheticist idealism seemed stronger than ever, but his unshakeable liberalism also meant that the freedom of art was even more important than the cult of beauty. As a result, he included the uncompromising works of the young Oskar Kokoschka in the exhibition. Although the Kunstschau marked the greatest triumph of the Klimt group—the "Stylists," as they were labelled by contemporaries—it also marked the end of the period in art that they had dominated. But for the moment the air rang with praise, for the best works in Klimt's golden style were on show. *The Kiss* was an instant success—so much so that it was purchased by the government. In *The Kiss* the lovers are elevated to the realm of religious iconography. The gold background is reminiscent of Byzantine mosaics, as are the glittering ornamental robes. The painting was a representation of the eternal Adam and Eve, a sacred picture of love. The model for Adam was said to be Klimt himself, holding Emilie Flöge in his arms. The seemingly idyllic moment in Paradise is highly ambivalent. There is also something anxious and claustrophobic in the canvas. The cushion of flowers on which the woman is kneeling breaks off abruptly at the edge of an abyss. Moreover, there are inconsistencies in the composition: The woman is kneeling, but the man seems to be standing and the heads are level. The relationship of the two bodies is completely subsumed in the overwhelming flow of ornamentation in their robes. The embrace is not fulfilled, the hands seem to grasp convulsively rather than caress. Only the woman's face is visible, but it resembles a mask, without personalized features. The whole picture is almost as stylized as an icon.

Besides *The Kiss*, two other allegories of mankind were shown at the 1908 exhibition: *Hope II* (see page 61) and *Danae* (see page 52). The second version of *Hope* was a less offensive representation of pregnancy than its predecessor (painted in 1903), without its fierce naturalism. The mother figure is seen here in the middle of a group of worshipping women against a background of golden space. Like *The Kiss*, it is designed as an icon. The structure of the narrow, figurative strip in front of an abstract background closely resembles the composition of *The Three Ages*. As in the first version of *Hope*, Death is placed close to the pregnant woman, but warm colors and a meditative atmosphere suggest a more optimistic interpretation of the same theme. The painting was also called *Vision*, *Fertility*, and *Legend*, and these alternative titles bear witness to Klimt's mellowing attitude. As for *Danae*, there can be few representations of the ecstasy of love as succesful as this. Klimt depicts here the mystery of female sexuality—a fashionable subject at that time, but usually treated with voyeuristic prurience—with unambiguous naturalism; at the same time he conveyed an enchantingly idealized aestheticism that enhanced the merely erotic. The model recalls the red-haired femmes fatales, the naiads and nymphs of earlier works, and the evil powers of the *Beethoven Frieze*. Beside the curled flesh of the body pours a torrent of gold coins, the golden rain of Zeus, mixed with gold spermatozoa. The patterns on the dark purple veil shimmer, Danae's hair flames in russet hues—the whole picture radiates eroticism. This effect is enhanced by the close-up focus on the looming immanent flesh of woman. Here is the woman as the bearer of the secret of life itself, but she is also Klimt's favorite theme, the epitome of sensual beauty. Women were truly the focus of Klimt's curiosity, as an artist and a man, a curiosity that led him to depict them boldy in unorthodox poses and situtations, even as lesbians, as in the two versions of *Watersnakes* (see page 41).

At the 1909 Kunstschau Klimt presented a second version on the theme of Salome. Here the heroine is a more vigorous figure than in the first painting. The enveloping ornamentation of spirals, small colored patches, and ovals heightens the dangerous dynamism of a decadent society woman (see page 72). This *Judith II (Salome)* marked Klimt's first confrontation with Expressionism. By then his style was reaching a point where no further development was possible. While Vienna was celebrating his works at the exhibition, Klimt was struggling with a new allegory on a philosophical theme, *Death and Life*, also entitled *Death and Love* (see page 81). This composition was completed only in 1916. It returns to the ideas of *Medicine*, but it is also a reflection of developments in Klimt's style and changes in his view of the world. Originally the eternal cycle of birth, life, and death was painted on a gold background. Opposite Death on the left, Life was represented by a human pyramid consisting of an embracing couple together with the female figure of *The Three Ages*. In the final version, the background is cold blue, and Death has become a far more menacing figure. It seems that the painting entitled *The Virgin* (see page 76) played a decisive role in the changes toward the final realization of *Death and Life*. The peripheral figures in this final version bear a resemblance to the figures in *The Virgin*, and the gold background has been replaced by a multicolored one. The really interesting question, therefore, is what were the causes of the changes evident from about 1909 onward? Why change something that was already a complete vision in 1909 to something that was so different in both in form and content?

Shortly before the opening of the 1908 exhibition, Ludwig Hevesi visited Klimt's studio and reported that the master seemed to have aged. In contemporary photographs he looks much older than his forty-six years, and tired. The fierce struggle around the university paintings, emotional strains, and bitter disappointments had made him prematurely old. Once more the exhibition made the original dream of the Secession a brief reality: an ideal harmony formed by the Künstlerschaft, an imaginary community of artists and connoisseurs, as Klimt defined it in his opening remarks at the exhibition. This great show of Austrian art was a demonstration that the Künstlerschaft was a strong alliance. In reality, there was a harmonious cooperation only between the Stylists (Klimt's group), the members of the Wiener Werkstätte, and a few rich patrons of art. The marriage between the public at large and the artists was tenuous and could not be maintained. The concept of Künstlerschaft itself, even in its theoretical form, was outmoded. By 1907 artists in Paris, Munich, and Moscow had given up their dream of harmony and the reform of life through the magic of almighty art. The turbulent time before the First World War produced a dramatic heightening of expression with harsh effects. The art world was filled with desperate warnings about the future of the world, or mystical theories

LADY WITH HAT AND FEATHERBOA, 1909
Oil on canvas, 27⅛″ × 21⅝″ (69 × 55 cm). Oesterreichische Galerie, Vienna

PORTRAIT OF ADELE BLOCH-BAUER II, 1912
Oil on canvas, 74¾″ × 47¼″ (190 × 120 cm)
Oesterreichische Galerie, Vienna

PORTRAIT OF MÄDA PRIMAVESI, 1912
Oil on canvas, 59″ × 43½″ (150 × 110.5 cm). The Metropolitan Museum of Art, New York
Gift of André and Clara Mertens, in memory of her mother, Jenny Pulitzer Steiner

And eschatologies that had little to do with social reform through the arts. How could Klimt adapt to this changed environment? The 1908 and 1909 Vienna exhibitions were a triumph for Klimt, but they also marked the end of his role as a leader. Although he had been the first to champion the works of Oskar Kokoschka and Egon Schiele, he understood that these younger men were pursuing different goals. As he put it in his interview with Bertha Zuckerkandl: "Youth does not understand me any more. They are heading in a different direction. I do not even know whether they value me at all. The usual fate of the artist has overtaken me earlier than most. Youth always destroys first that which already exists. However, since this is always the case, I bear them no grudge.[1]

THE CRISIS: CONFRONTATION WITH EXPRESSIONISM AND FAUVISM

By 1909 a new generation of artists was growing up in Vienna. They regarded Klimt as their idol, yet they brought a markedly different approach to both art and life. Among them were Schiele and Kokoschka, who were first influenced by Klimt, and in turn influenced him later. At the 1909 exhibition Klimt was dazzled by the works of such masters as Vincent Van Gogh, Edvard Munch, Lovis Corinth, Pierre Bonnard, and Henri Matisse. He was most stirred by the Expressionists among them, and in October he travelled to Paris, where more artistic wonders awaited him. He fell under the spell of Henri de Toulouse-Lautrec, and he was at once fascinated by Fauvism. As a consequence, he suffered a crisis of artistic confidence. He realized that his golden style could no longer express profound ideas about life. He may also have suffered the anguish peculiar to those who regard themselves as part of the avant-garde and suddenly become aware that they

(1) Bertha Zuckerkandl. "Einiges über Klimt," *Volkszeitung*, Vienna, 2.6.1936. Quoted in C. M. Nebehay, *op. cit.*, p. 256.

are bringing up the rear. Klimt needed time to absorb these many new experiences, and the paintings of this period betray the influence of several artists. Paintings such as *The Avenue of Schloss Kammer Park* (see page 75) show the powerful presence of Van Gogh. The flat decorativeness of earlier wood and garden pictures gives way to more solid masses, and the lines are much stronger. But unlike Van Gogh, who imbued nature with an elemental passion that made it human and filled it with existential suffering, Klimt emphasized the peaceful harmony of creation. This sense of balance—with an implicit melancholy—was also characteristic of his later townscapes, in which, according to Johannes Dobai, there are even traces of incipient Cubism.[1] The 1909 landscapes combine water, vegetation, and buildings. Man is still excluded, but signs of his presence reflect a balance between his world and nature. The color schemes owe something to Fauvism, but the harsh colors of the French school are refined into a soft harmony of green, red, and yellow tones. Klimt's allegiance to mystical pantheism welled up in his landscapes. They were personal expressions of his reverence

(1) Johannes Dobai, *op. cit.*, p. 264.

JUDITH II (Salome), 1909
Oil on canvas
70 × 18⅛"
(178 × 46 cm)
Galleria d'Arte Moderna
Venice
◁

Young Girl Naked, c. 1916
Pencil drawing
22⁷/₁₆" × 14¾" (57 × 37,5 cm)
Kunstmuseum Berne

UNTERACH AM ATTERSEE, 1915
Oil on canvas, 43⅜″ × 43⅜″ (110 × 110 cm)
Residenzgalerie, Salzburg

AVENUE OF SCHLOSS KAMMER PARK, 1912
Oil on canvas, 43⅜″ × 43⅜″ (110 × 110 cm)
Oesterreichische Galerie, Vienna

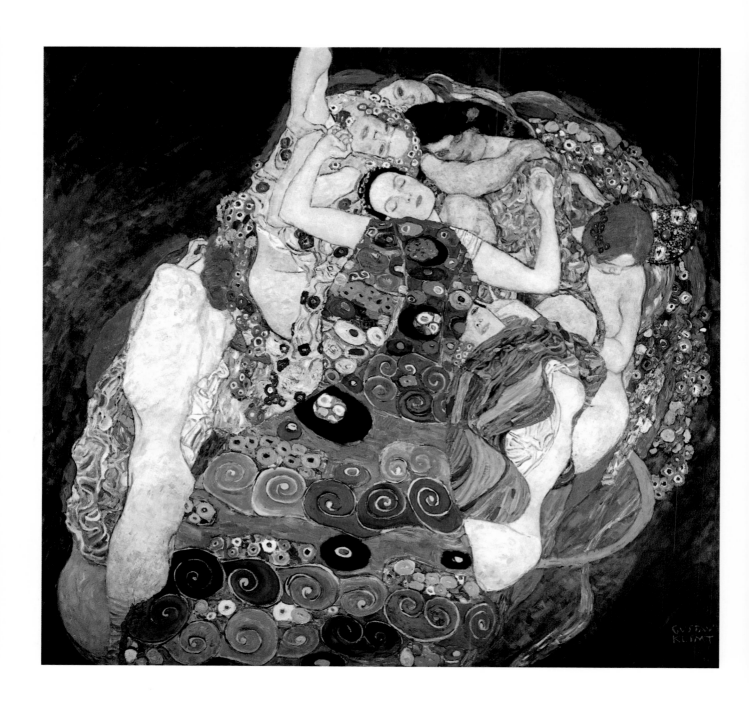

THE VIRGIN, 1913
Oil on canvas, 73¾″ × 78⅝″ (190 × 200 cm)
Narodni Galerie, Prague

for the beauty of life, equally present in the smallest flower and the great cosmic cycle of nature. Klimt seemed to propose humanized nature as a refuge from man-made society. Nature could not be changed by the arts, but it could be enriched by the intimate vision created by true masterpieces.

Lady with Hat and Featherboa (see page 69) was the first painting to mark such a change in Klimt's style, and it showed the influence of Toulouse-Lautrec. This portrait of an appealing society woman could have been painted ten years earlier, except that the broken brushstroke is characteristic of Expressionism. Gold and geometric ornamentation had vanished from Klimt's work, and there was a return to realism although a strong decorative element remained. The change could not be accounted for solely by the journey to Paris, and a later one to Spain. The 1908 Vienna exhibition had already confronted Klimt with Kokoschka's uncompromising brutalism and the psychological cruelties of Schiele's work. This would have been sufficient to demonstrate that art in Vienna had changed dramatically. Although Klimt could never renounce aestheticism, he was sensitive and open-minded enough to assimilate something from this new and somewhat threatening quarter. He abandoned his golden style not only because

THE BRIDE, 1917-18
Oil on canvas (here in black and white)
65¼″ × 73¾″
(166 × 190 cm)
Oesterreichische Galerie
Vienna
(Private collection)

Reclining Naked Woman, n.d.
Lead, blue and red pencil, white chalk, 14⅜″ × 21⅝″ (36.7 × 55.9 cm)
Historisches Museum der Stadt Wien, Vienna

the young Expressionists had made it anachronistic, but also because it had led to a stiffness and stylization which limited possibilities for psychological expression.

THE FAUVIST PERIOD

The basic genres of Klimt's art remained unchanged up to the time of his death—portraits, landscapes, and allegories. In his last period, however, these familiar genres were treated with greater expression of feelings and the pictures became less abstract. Human types were no longer disguised in the context of myth or fairy tale. They appeared before the viewer in unvarnished reality. Thus the golden *Watersnakes* of 1904-1909 became lesbian beauties in the painting entitled *Friends* (see page 91). In Klimt's late canvases, large colorful patterns or Oriental motifs dominate the background to the point of overwhelming the figures while at the same time expressing particular aspects of their character. His last important portraits feature a very low horizon, thus putting the standing model on a "pedestal"; the coloring is bright and luminous, but without gold; the face of the sitter is intense and full of character.

In 1912 Klimt painted a second portrait of *Adele Bloch-Bauer* (see page 70), which is quite different from the first version. The anatomical reality of the slender figure is completely remodelled by the draping of a bluish-gray stole, in addition to a huge black hat, so that she herself becomes a two-dimensional ornament. The painting is a tapestry featuring irregular figurative patterns and asymmetrical stripes of color, creating an impression of uncertainty and nervous movement. This restlessness affects the viewer's association with the model, whose blank face and clawing hands suggest an anxious personality. The portrait of nine-year-old *Mäda Primavesi* (see page 71) was painted in the same year as *Adele Bloch-Bauer II*, but it depicts a very different personality—an alert, self-confident girl with a strong character, which is by no means subdued by the vivid patterns in the white carpet and mauve background. Elisabeth Bachofen-Echt was the daugter of August Lederer, the loyal patron who had helped Klimt buy back the university paintings. Klimt painted her as he had her mother fifteen years earlier,

Reclining Woman, c. 1913-1914
Blue pencil, 14½" × 22" (36.9 × 56 cm). Historisches Museum der Stadt Wien, Vienna

wearing a white dress. The thin body of this young bride-to-be is also very stylized, like that of Adele Bloch-Bauer — she is molded into the shape of a delicate vase. The effect, however, is not that of a whimsical arabesque, but of sophisticated beauty. Her apparent fragility is balanced by the ornamental triangle on the wall behind her, which protects her like a magic cloak — and indeed has its origins in traditional Chinese "dragon cloaks" which were supposed to bring good luck. Alice Strobl has unraveled the iconography on the wall, with earth, sea, sky, dragons, and clouds.[1] The diminutive figures were copied from an imported Chinese vase, and they bring a touch of humor to an otherwise hieratically severe composition that is dominated hy the model's large, intelligent black eyes. The portrait of *Friedericke Maria Beer* achieves a different effect. The sitter was a rich young patron of the arts who had already commissioned Schiele to paint her portrait. In Klimt's painting (see page 84) her intelligence and strength of character are made evident by the frontal pose. As in the portrait of *Elisabeth Bachofen-Echt*, the horizon is low, so that the viewer looks up at the model as if she were on a pedestal. She wears a daringly exotic dress with large patterns from a Wiener Werkstätte design. Klimt drew many sketches for this portrait; they radiate peace, yet the final picture is disquieting, because of its highly colored and animated background. Half-life-size figures are taken from the same Oriental vase as in the portrait of *Elisabeth Bachofen-Echt*, but they are engaged in warfare on the wall behind the sitter; their swords clash exactly behind her static figure, a jarring collision juxtaposed to her evident calm and intransigence. Later Friedericke Maria Beer denied that this aspect of the painting had any symbolic meaning,[2] but one cannot help remembering that this canvas was painted during the First World War, in 1916.

In his final period Klimt painted two great allegories with similar themes: *The Virgin* (see page 76) and *The Bride* (see page 77). The latter was to remain unfinished. One or two other works could also be included in the allegory genre — such as *Baby* (see page 85) and *Adam and Eve* (see page 88). The former has considerable charm, with the baby peeping out of a pyramid of colored clothes with small black, intensely vivid eyes. *Adam and Eve* also remained unfinished. This was the last example of Klimt's lovers, and it showed stark differences in treatment from previous versions. The Rubenesque bulk of Eve fills the whole canvas; she gazes at the viewer with an impersonal doll-like stare. Adam is a passive figure, his eyes closed and his head turned to the side. He seems to be diminished and controlled by the massive contours of Eve, as if the female principle is the one that rules. While the dominant female remained an important theme throughout Klimt's works, the enigmatic and threatening femmes fatales were not to be found after 1910. A softer female type came to the fore, who was closer to nature and plants than the baleful semi-mythological vamps of the Secessionist years.

(1) Alice Strobl, *op. cit.*, p. 91.
(2) Quoted in Alessandra Comini, *op. cit.*, pp. 17-18; C. M. Nebehay, *op. cit.*, pp. 267-268.

DEATH AND LIFE, 1908-1916
Oil on canvas, 70¹/₁₆″ × 77⅞″ (178 × 198 cm)
From "Die Kunst" XXVII, 1913

Since *Death and Life* Klimt had used only pure colors, and he sculpted the figures in his canvases in soft rounded contours. An aging, tired master, he had abandoned the task of depicting the great drama of the life cycle, preferring to paint instead the glorious moments of beauty and youth. This may have been the natural result of his growing awareness of his own mortality. Over and again he tried to catch the great moment in life, the ecstasy of love, and fix it on paper or on canvas. In *The Virgin* he set himself the task of showing the stages in the emotional and sensual development of a young girl as she becomes a woman. The girl is depicted from above; she is surrounded by swirling colorful ribbons and items of clothing. She seems lost in a dream. Parts of female bodies emerge in different postures from the ornamental background—incarnations of the dream of mature womanhood. The mass of bodies and ornaments is three-dimensional and it seems to revolve slowly in space, tumbling on its way to an unknown destination.

Although the outbreak of the First World War in 1914 must have deeply affected Klimt, it had no noticeable effect on his paintings. The death of his mother in 1915, however, introduced a markedly somber note. The three landscapes painted at the time evoke a dreamy melancholy. Ornamentation disappeared from the paintings and dark tones prevailed, as in the now lost portraits of two old women. By 1916 the crisis seemed to have passed, and Klimt returned to the celebration of the glorious abundance of nature and female beauty. He painted many landscapes and sensual half-figure female portraits. In a final burst of creative energy, Klimt began work on his last great composition, *The Bride*. It is an enigmatic picture and has much in common with *The Virgin*. Dobai has suggested that the figure clad in a blue robe, standing in the middle of the picture, is the bride, while the surrounding figures might be stages of her hallucination.[1] The precise interpretation of the work's iconography is yet to be completed, but the one-hundred-and-forty preparatory sketches show the genesis of the composition. The bridegroom's face can be seen among the swirling figures of the final painting. The female creature on the right may represent ecstasy and fulfilment. *The Bride* does not lend itself to schematic and logical analysis.[2] It is close to a Freudian dream, whose images are arbitrary and personal, though no less significant for being so. Its strength lies in this disturbingly fragmented and vivid quality. It points to the strong tensions inherent in Klimt's creative imagination. Dynamic and expressive use of color was always accompanied by playfully calligraphic ornaments; hence, this attempt to depict the heights of ecstasy is marked by contrived stylization. This creates an alienating effect, because it reveals the analytical planning behind the artistic process.

Most of the large canvases of Klimt's late years remained unfinished: On January 11, 1918, Klimt was felled by a stroke, and he died on February 6, only six months before the collapse

(1) Fritz Novotny and Johannes Dobai. *Gustav Klimt*. Salzburg: Galerie Welz, 1968, 1975, p. 126.
(2) Marian Bisanz-Prakken, *op. cit.*, in R. Waissenberger, ed., *Traum und Wirklichkeit*, Salzburg: Galerie Welz, 1984, pp. 119-120.

of the Austro-Hungarian Empire. In the
magnificent flowering of that complex and
doomed culture he had been a great
genius — to the age its man, and to the
man his freedom.

KLIMT'S DRAFTSMANSHIP

Klimt was one of greatest draftsmen in
the history of European art. This was
universally acknowledged among his
contemporaries, and his drawings were
often more highly valued than his paintings.
Sketching came to him as naturally as
drawing breath. His graphic work, recently
documented by Alice Strobl, runs to over
three thousand items, which Strobl related
to his major paintings, thus establishing
their chronology as well as delineating the
development in Klimt's style.[1]

The main theme of this enormous œuvre
was the female body. The few male figures
are either adjuncts to women or necessary
components of the great allegorical
compositions. Klimt's choice of models was
determined by the changing contemporary
ideal of female beauty. Above all, he loved
to depict a delicately boyish type of woman
with a hint of androgyny. He drew sketches
that are among the finest examples of turn-
of-the-century erotic art. His working
method ensured that the sketches would be
very natural. As in Auguste Rodin's studio,
two or three nude models moved around as
he worked, and they were seldom asked to

(1) Alice Strobl, *op. cit.*, vol. I-III.

*Study for the Portrait
of Maria Beer-Monti, c. 1915
Pencil drawing on wrapping paper
23¾" × 11⅜" (60.4 × 29 cm)
Neue Galerie der Stadt Linz.
Wolfgang Gurlitt Museum, Austria*

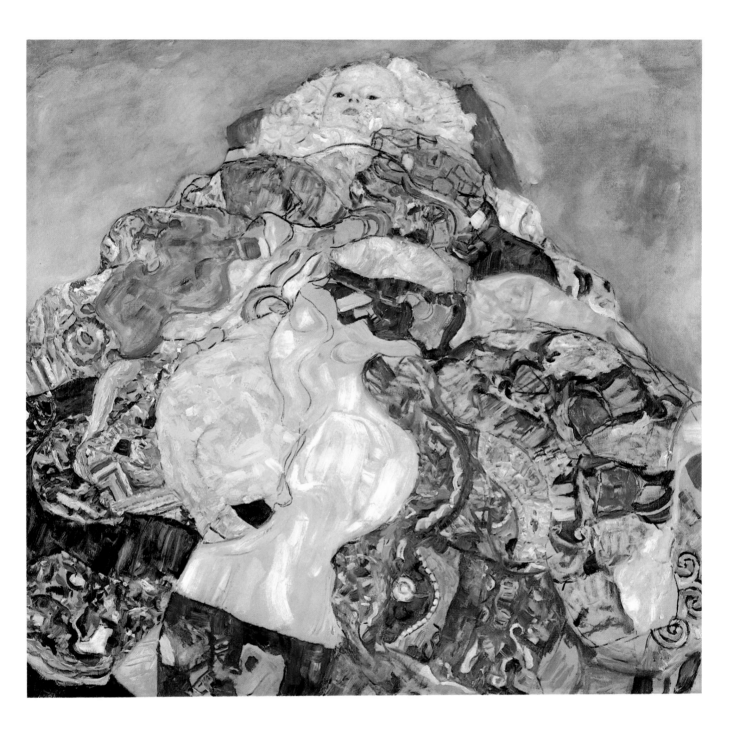

◁

FRIEDERICKE MARIA BEER, 1916
Oil on canvas
66⅛″ × 51⅛″ (168 × 130 cm)
Collection: Markus and
Felicja Mizne, Monte-Carlo

BABY, 1917-1918. Oil on canvas
45⅝″ × 43½″ (110.9 × 110.4 cm)
National Gallery of Art, Washington, D.C.
Gift of Otto and Franziska Kallir with the help
of the Carol and Edwin Fullinwider Fund

Dancer, 1917
Lead, 19½" × 12⅝" (49.6 × 32.4 cm)
Albertina, Vienna

adopt a specific pose. Instead, Klimt drew swift sketches whenever he caught a spontaneous movement or position of the body. Thus, he captured the female form, sitting or lying on a sofa or a bed, in all its unassuming natural sensuality. The same models were also used in his great allegories.

Klimt's drawings underwent several changes in style. Early on he abandoned the precise dry style of the academy, retaining only its tendency to idealize. This was heightened by overly stylized proportions and fine colors, as in *Allegory of Sculpture* (see page 7), which is reminiscent of French Salon paintings. From the early 1890s on, his technique featured more and more elements drawn from Art Nouveau. For a while he worked in the international graphic style that was typical of the time — thick parallel lines of black chalk that gave a soft relief to objects and figures and expressed the most delicate gradations of light and dark. A large group of fine portraits of women were executed in this manner. They strongly resembled those of French and English mood Symbolism. Klimt was also influenced by the calligraphic decoration of Greek vases. In the early years of the Secession, and especially in the works he did for "Ver Sacrum," different influences could be detected, including those of Jan Toorop, Aubrey Beardsley, and Auguste Rodin. The preparatory drawings for the *Beethoven Frieze* and *Jurisprudence* formed a cohesive group of their own. They were executed on tan wrapping paper with charcoal or black chalk, featuring strong fluid contours with intermittent shading.

Around 1903 Klimt seemed to have found his most satisfactory medium. Previously he had used charcoal, black chalk, crayon, even pen and ink, without paying much attention to the paper surface. From 1903 he used almost exclusively graphite pencil on fine Japan paper. This change coincided with a change of technique — unnecessary details, perspective, and shading were eliminated. The drawings were made of a few gentle lines that were suggestive rather than complete.

Between 1905 and 1907 Eastern mysticism in religion, philosophy, and art made its deepest impression on Klimt. Outlines became more angular and expressions or gestures associated with Eastern rituals occured frequently. From 1907 until about 1912, Klimt's work was strongly two-dimensional.

Klimt's drawings are erotic, but they lack the cynicism of Jules Pascin and the detachment of Toulouse-Lautrec. He relished eroticism at its most sophisticated and had a taste for its aesthetic decadence. It was he who drew masterly illustrations for Lucian's "Dialogues of the Hetaerae," which are gems of voyeuristic expertise.[1] Throughout his different periods Klimt always viewed his models aesthetically, even when he depicted the most daring and deliberately provocative poses, focusing on erogenous zones. There is no cruelty or vulgarity in his works, however, much his critics tried to label the erotic drawings exhibited privately in 1910 as pornographic. His outlook was consistently one of gentleness, sympathy, and a sensitivity toward any intimate aspect of the psyche.

In 1909 Klimt's draftsmanship changed, as did his style in painting. The works of such varied artists as Toulouse-Lautrec and El Greco made a deep impression on him. His drawings became progressively less two-dimensional. The third dimension was introduced by intriguing foreshortening, diagonal gestures of the models, and dramatic broken lines. The earlier calm, even languid scenes gave way to passion or ecstasy. In spite of these changes, Klimt's late drawings were not Expressionist in style. He always tempered the violence inherent in Expressionism with clear lines,

Two Studies from the Nude, c. 1913-1915
Lead, 22¼" × 14⁵⁄₁₆" (56.6 × 37 cm)
Eidgenössische Technische
Hochschule, Zurich. Graphische Sammlung

(1) *Die Hetärengespräche des Lukian.* Translated by Franz Blei. With fifteen drawings by Gustav Klimt. Leipzig: Julius Zeitler, 1907.

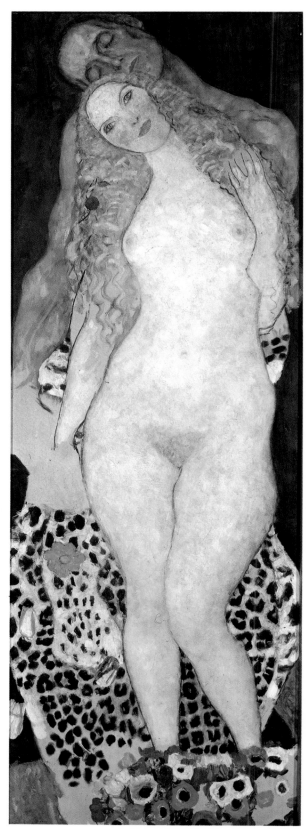

ADAM AND EVA (unfinished), 1917-1918
Oil on canvas, 67⅞″ × 32⅝″ (175 × 60 cm)
Oesterreichische Galerie, Vienna

precise craftsmanship, and a genuine respect for a perfection of style. These preoccupations were at the heart of his aestheticism, and they removed from his work the painful physical immediacy characteristic of pictures by Kokoschka and Schiele.

EPILOGUE

> There is no self-portrait of me. I am not interested in any individual personality as the "subject of a picture," but rather in other human beings, above all female, and still more in other phenomena.[1]

This statement by Klimt is more than a little enigmatic. What were those phenomena that interested him more than women? If the answer is to be found in his work, the paintings that meant the most to him were those on which he was prepared to lavish care and love. They were philosophical allegories, in which he could explore the ultimate questions about man's existence. He viewed these philosopical and psychological themes in terms of artistic problems that had to be solved through painting. All that he felt, heard, or read was grist to the artistic mill. His greatness lay in an amazing ability to impose visual immediacy on complicated and esoteric images. His allegories unfold their themes around the great cycle of life and death, based on an eclectic selection of contemporary antirational philosophies. Klimt saw life as ever threatened by death and decay, but in spite of this pessimistic view his works radiate wisdom and natural sensuousness born out of joy in the beauty of life and its eternal renewal. He believed that man could find happiness in sensual pleasure and balanced relationships. The force of life seemed to be stronger for him than the threat of death. Life was the dynamic cosmic power of the universe, and it could not be defeated, even if man as an individual was doomed to destruction. The secret of this survival was love, a mystical force rescuing life from death through an endless chain of individual mortal lives. Klimt evoked constantly the mystery of love, that essence of existence. The fecundity of women—who on the surface were often mere objects of sexuality—was in fact the source of their sacred strength. Klimt was perhaps the last great Symbolist who hoped to embrace a cosmic view of the universe in a single vision. Most of the late-nineteenth-century Symbolists, such as Fernand Khnopff and Gustave Moreau, were pessimists. Klimt was the exception. He loved beauty for its own sake, and the whole fundamental human process of loving and being loved. He could make peace with a philosophy in which the individual was doomed to a brief flowering before vanishing once more into the eternal cycle of nature. At the turn of the century, when European intellectuals were struggling bitterly for the rights of the individual and when the main theme in Austrian literature was the existential loneliness of man, Klimt reduced man's

---

(1) Quoted in Christian M. Nebehay, *op. cit.*, p. 40.

role to that of an anonymous carrier of the message of life—and he was reconciled to a peaceful acceptance of this destiny.

Perhaps this unusual stance enabled Klimt to subordinate his own happiness to the demands of his art. He could preserve his harmonious humanistic view of the world in an age and an environment in which all the great intellectuals—Hugo von Hofmannsthal, Karl Kraus, Rainer-Maria Rilke, Franz Kafka, Robert Musil—were deep pessimists. As they contemplated the last days of mankind with a mixture of cynicism and anguish, Klimt was re-creating the splendor of a lost Eden, the golden dream of aestheticism.

We wish to thank the owners of the pictures reproduced herein,
as well as those collectors who did not want their names mentioned.
Our special thanks go to the Galerie Welz in Salzburg for their kind assistance.

FRIENDS, 1917. Oil on canvas
Destroyed by fire in 1945. 39″ × 39″ (99 × 99 cm)
Photo: Courtesy Galerie Welz, Salzburg

GIRL'S HEAD TURNED LEFT, 1915
Lead, red and brown pencil, 14″ × 13%₁₆″ (35.5 × 34.5 cm)
Liechtensteinische Staatliche Kunstsammlung, Vaduz

BIOGRAPHY

1862 Born on July 14, in Baumgarten, to a lower-middle-class family of Moravian peasant stock. His father was a goldsmith and engraver.

1876-1883 Won a scholarship to study at the Vienna School of Arts and Crafs with Ferdinand Julius Laufberger. He was still in school when he began working with his painter brother Ernst and his friend Franz Matsch, for the architectural firm Fellner and Helmer.

1880 Paintings for the ceilings at the Kurhaus in Karlovy Vary, with Ernst Klimt and Franz Matsch.

1881 Worked on a series entitled *Allegories and Emblems*, (German title: *Allegorien und Embleme*), for the Viennese publisher Martin Gerlach.

1883 Established an independent studio with Ernst Klimt and Franz Matsch.

1884 Strongly influenced by the work of Hans Makart.

1885 The Klimt studio was commissioned to decorate the Empress Elizabeth's villa near Vienna after designs by Makart.

1886-1888 The studio was commissioned to decorate the staircase, ceilings, and lunette of the new Burgtheater. Klimt was awarded the Gold Medal for this work.

1890 Was awarded the Emperor's Prize for his painting *The Old Burgtheater*. The studio began decoration of the staircase hall of the Vienna Museum of Art History.

1891 Joined the Künstlerhaus. His style began to change as he did further work decorating the Museum of Art History.

1892 The museum's wallpaintings received critical acclaim. His father died, followed by the death of his brother Ernst in December.

1893 Year of crisis. His appointment at the Academy of Fine Arts was not confirmed by the Ministry of Culture.

1894 Klimt and Matsch were commissioned to paint the ceiling of the University Aula. The Matsch-Klimt studio broke up.

1895 *Love* and *Music I.*

1896 Drew in a clearly Art Noveau style. Became friends with Carl Moll, Josef Hoffmann, and Otto Wagner.

1897 On April 3, the Vienna Secession was founded. Klimt was elected its first president and thus regarded as the leader of modern art in Austria. First landscapes painted at the Attersee. His portraits showed the influence of James Whistler.

1898 First Secession exhibition. Klimt designed the poster. The group's periodical, "Ver Sacrum," started publication. In November, at the second Secession exhibition, Klimt showed *Pallas Athena* and *Schubert at the Piano*.

1899 Finished the decoration of the music room at the Dumba mansion in Vienna. Painted *Nuda Veritas* in a Pointillist technique. Started work on *Philosophy*, the first panel for the University commission.

1900 Exhibited *Philosophy*. Eighty-seven University pro-fessors protested against the painting, which was awarded a Gold Medal in Paris.

1901 The second panel, *Medicine*, stirred such a scandal that critics and public were divided in two camps and the Ministry of Culture withdrew its support of Klimt.

1902 The Beethoven exhibition in the House of Secession. Klimt's frieze was so stylized and loaded with symbols that it failed to please the public and the art establishment.

1903 The beginning of Klimt's "golden style." His artist friends founded the Wiener Werkstätte. Retrospective exhibition of Klimt's work at the House of Secession in December.

1904 Tension grew between Klimt's group and the other members of the Secession. Klimt's drawings underwent significant changes in style.

1905 Klimt and his friends left the Secession. He bought back his University paintings from the Ministry of Culture. *Hope* and *The Three Ages (of Woman)* were exhibited in Berlin. He began to work on the Stoclet Friezes.

1906 *Portrait of Fritza Riedler*. Landscapes showing Van Gogh's influence. *Sunflower.*

1907 High point of Klimt's golden style: *Portrait of Adele Bloch-Bauer, Danae, Hope II*. Illustrations to Lucian's "Dialogues of the Hetaerae." The Stoclet frieze. Klimt and Egon Schiele became acquainted.

1908 Kunstschau exhibition in Vienna. Klimt's masterpiece, *The Kiss*, was purchased by the Austrian National Gallery. Kokoschka also showed his work at the Kunstschau.

1909 *Judith II* was shown at the second Vienna Kunstchau exhibition. In the fall, Klimt traveled to Paris, were he discovered the newest artistic trends there. His work betrayed the influence of Toulouse-Lautrec and the Fauves. *Lady with Hat and Featherboa.*

1910 Klimt's style changed, other colors replaced gold. *Death and Life.*

1911 International Exhibition in Rome. First prize for *Death and Life*. Klimt's friezes were installed in the Stoclet mansion in Brussels. He set up a new studio in Vienna, at Unter St. Veit.

1912 Highly decorative and colorful portraits influenced by Matisse. Klimt changed the background of *Death and Life* from gold to blue; see also *Avenue of Schloss Kammer Park, Mäda Primavesi.*

1913 *The Virgin* shown in Munich. Exhibition in Budapest.

1913 Exhibited with the Künstlerbund in Prague.

1915 His mother died. Klimt's palette darkened in tone. *Portrait of Barbara Flöge* and *Portrait of Charlotte Pulitzer.*

1916 Portrait with richly decorative patterns: *Friedericke Maria Beer, Friends.*

1917 Many new compositions and portraits of women. Started work on *The Bride, Adam and Eve.*

1918 Klimt died from cerebral haemorrhage on February 6. Many paintings remained unfinished.

EXHIBITIONS

1958 Staatliche Kunstalle, Baden-Baden. *Gustav Klimt and Egon Schiele*. Foreword by L. Zahn.

1959 Albertina, Vienna. *Gustav Klimt*. Memorial exhibitions.

1960 Ch.M. Nebehay Gallery, Vienna. *Gustav Klimt*. 40 drawings.
Arcade Gallery, London. *Thirty Drawings by Gustav Klimt*.

1962 Albertina, Vienna. *Gustav Klimt 1862-1918*. Memorial exhibition of drawings. Foreword by W. Koschatzky and A. Strobl, catalogue by A. Strobl.
Österreichische Galerie, Vienna. *Gustav Klimt*. 29 paintings.
Ch.M. Nebehay Gallery, Vienna. *Gustav Klimt*. 150 major drawings. Foreword by Ch.M. Nebehay.
Neue Galerie am Landesmuseum Joanneum, Graz. *Gustav Klimt*.

1964 Haus der Kunst, Munich. *Secession. European Art at the Turn of the Century*.
Galerie Welz, Salzburg. *Gustav Klimt*. Drawings.
Künstlerhaus, Vienna. *Vienna around 1900*.
Ch.M. Nebehay Gallery, Vienna. *Jugendstil and Secession. Graphics and Drawings 1880-1918*.
Winnipeg Art Gallery, Winnipeg. *Gustav Klimt. Drawings*. Catalogue by F. Eckhardt.

1965 Solomon R. Guggenheim Museum, New York. *Gustav Klimt and Egon Schiele*.
Marlbourgh Gallery, London. *Gustav Klimt, Paintings and Drawings*. Introduction by W. Fischer.
Galleria Stendhal, Milan. *Klimt, Drawings*. Introduction by G. Marchiori.

1967 Galerie St. Etienne, New York. *Gustav Klimt. Drawings*.
Ch. M. Nebehay Gallery, Vienna. *Gustav Klimt. 56 Drawings*.

1968 Albertina, Vienna. *Gustav Klimt and Egon Schiele*. Drawings and Watercolors. Essays by W. Koschatzky, A.P. Gütersloh, O. Benesch, E. Mitsch, and A. Strobl.
Ch.M. Nebehay Gallery, Vienna. *Gustav Klimt. Drawings and Documentation*.

1970 Galerie St. Etienne, New York. *Gustav Klimt, Drawings*. Introduction to the catalogue by G. Glueck.

1971 Royal Academy of Arts, London. *Vienna Secession, Art Nouveau to 1970*.
Künstlerhaus, Thurn u. Taxis Palace, Bregenz. *Jugendstil - Vienna Secession*.

1972 Haus der Kunst, Munich. *World Cultures and Modern Art*. Catalogue by S. Wickmann.
Arnoldi-Livie, Munich. *Gustav Klimt*.

1973 Piccadilly Gallery, London - Spencer A. Samuels Gallery, New York. *Gustav Klimt*. Introduction and notes by J. Dobai.
Galerie im Taxispalais, Innsbruck - Kulturhaus, Graz. *Gustav Klimt - Egon Schiele*. Drawings and watercolors. Catalogue by O. Breicha.

1974 Ch.M. Nebehay Gallery, Vienna. *Gustav Klimt*. Drawings and posters for the Secession.
Galleria I Portici, Torino. *Gustav Klimt and Vienna 1900*. Drawings, pastels and watercolors.
Galleria Ceraia, Milan. *Gustav Klimt and Vienna 1900, drawings, pastel, and watercolors*.

1976 Ch.M. Nebehay Gallery, Vienna. *Gustav Klimt*. Illustrated books, graphics, watercolors, and drawings.
Folkwang Museum, Essen. *Gustav Klimt - Drawings from the Albertina and from private collections*. Catalogue by A. Strobl.
Galerie Pabst, Munich, Vienna. *Gustav Klimt*. Drawings.

1977 Galerie Negru, Paris. *Gustav Klimt. Drawings*. Introduction to the catalogue by S. Sabarsky.

1978 Galerie Würthle, Vienna. *Gustav Klimt*. Drawings.
Galerie im Stadthaus, Klagenfurt - Kulturhaus, Graz - Museumspavillon in the Mirabell Gardens, Salzburg - Neue Galerie, Linz. *Gustav Klimt*. Drawings.

1980 Fischer Fine Art Ltd, London. *Vienna. Turn-of-the-century Art and Design*.
Galerie St. Etienne, New York. *Gustav Klimt - Egon Schiele*. Foreword by T.M. Messer, introduction by A. Comini, and catalogue by Jane Kallir.

1981 Palais des Beaux-Arts, Brussels. *Klimt - Schiele - Kokoschka*. Works on paper.
Kunsthalle, Hamburg. *Experiment Weltuntergang, Vienna 1900*. Catalogue by W. Hofmann.
Isetan Museum of Art, Tokyo. *Gustav Klimt*. Selection and introduction by S. Sabarsky.

1984 Palazzo della Permanente, Milan. *Gustav Klimt*. 100 drawings. Exhibition organized by S. Sabarsky.
Biennale, Venice. *Vienna 1900 - Art and Culture*. Catalogue by M. Marchetti.

1985 Künstlerhaus, Vienna. *Traum und Wirklichkeit*. Catalogue by R. Waissenberger.

1986 Centre national d'art et de culture Georges Pompidou, Paris. *Vienne 1880-1938: L'Apocalypse Joyeuse*. Catalogue ed. by J. Clair.
Museum of Modern Art, New York. *Vienna 1900: Art, Architecture, and Design*. Catalogue by K. Varnedoe.

SELECTED BIBLIOGRAPHY

WRITINGS BY KLIMT

Gustav Klimt. Eine Dokumentation. Edited by Christian M. Nebehay. Vienna: Galerie Ch.M. Nebehay, 1969.

BOOKS ILLUSTRATED BY KLIMT

LUCIAN. *Hetärengespräche.* Translated into German by Franz Blei. Fifteen drawings by Klimt. Leipzig: Julius Zeitler, 1907.

VERLAINE, Paul. *Femmes.* Six drawings by Gustav Klimt. The Dandy Books, n.d.

CATALOGUES RAISONNÉS

NOVOTNY, Fritz and DOBAI, Johannes. *Gustav Klimt,* catalogue raisonné of the paintings. Salzburg: Galerie Welz, 1967, 1975.

STROBL, Alice. *Gustav Klimt. Die Zeichnungen,* catalogue raisonné of the drawings. 3 vols. Salzburg: Galerie Welz, 1980-1984.

WORKS ON KLIMT

BAHR, Hermann. *Rede über Klimt.* Vienna: Wiener Verlag, n.d. (1901).

BAHR, Hermann. *Gegen Klimt.* Vienna, Leipzig: J. Eisenstein, 1903.

BAHR, Hermann. *Gustav Klimt. 50 Handzeichnungen.* Leipzig, Vienna: Thyros Verlag, 1922.

BAHR, Hermann and ALTENBERG, Peter. *Das Werk Gustav Klimts.* Leipzig, Vienna: Hugo Heller, (1914), 1918.

BAÜMER, Angelica. *Gustav Klimt: Frauen.* Salzburg: Galerie Welz, 1985.

BISANZ-PRAKKEN, Marian. *Der Beethovenfries.* Salzburg: Residenz Verlag, 1977.

BREICHA, Otto. *Gustav Klimt. Die Goldene Pforte.* Salzburg: Galerie Welz, 1978.

COMINI, Alessandra. *Gustav Klimt.* London: Thames and Hudson; New York: Braziller, 1975, 1981.

DOBAI, Johannes. *Das Frühwerk Gustav Klimts.* Unpublished doctoral dissertation, University of Vienna, 1958.

DOBAI, Johannes. "Die Landschaft in der Sicht von Gustav Klimt. Ein Essay", *Klimt Studien.* Salzburg: Galerie Welz, 1978.

DOBAI, Johannes. *Gustav Klimt. Die Landschaften.* Salzburg: Galerie Welz, 1981.

EISLER, Max. *Gustav Klimt.* Vienna: Austrian State Printing Office, 1920. English language edition, 1921.

EISLER, Max. *Gustav Klimt, An Aftermath.* Translated by B.W. Tucker. Vienna: Austrian State Printing Office, 1931.

GILHOFER-MAPPE. *Gustav Klimt. 25 Handzeichnungen.* With 25 drawings from the Erich Lederer Collection, Geneva. Vienna: Gilhofer and Ranschburg, 1919.

HATLE, Ingomar. *Gustav Klimt, ein Wiener Maler des Jugendstils.* Unpublished doctoral dissertation, University of Graz, 1955.

HEVESI, Ludwig. *Acht Jahre Secession* (March 1897 - June 1905). Vienna: Carl Konegen, 1906.

HEVESI, Ludwig. *Altkunst - Neukunst. Wien 1894-1908.* Vienna: Carl Konegen, 1909.

HOFMANN, Werner. *Gustav Klimt.* Milan: Fratelli Fabbri, 1967. Translated by Inge Goodwin, Greenwich, Connecticut: New York Graphic Society, 1971.

HOFMANN, Werner. *Gustav Klimt und die Wiener Jahrhundertwende.* Salzburg: Galerie Welz, 1970.

NEBEHAY, Christian M. *Gustav Klimt. Sein Leben nach zeitgenössischen Berichten und Quellen.* Munich, dtv, 1976.

PIRCHAN, Emil. *Gustav Klimt, ein Künstler aus Wien.* Leipzig, Vienna: Wallishauer Verlag, 1942; rev. ed., Vienna: Berland Verlag, 1956.

SCHORSKE, Carl E. "Gustav Klimt: Painting and the Crisis of the Liberal Ego" *Fin-de-siècle Vienna. Politics and Culture.* New York: Albert A. Knopf, 1980, pp. 208-278.

STROBL, Alice. *Gustav Klimt. Zeichnungen und Gemälde.* Salzburg: Galerie Welz, 1962; rev. ed. in German and English, 1965.

STROBL, Alice. "Zu den Fakultätsbildern von Gustav Klimt" *Albertina Studien,* II (1964), pp. 138-169.

STROBL, Alice. "Gustav Klimt in der Kritik seiner Zeit" *Die Weltkunst,* XLVI (May 1976), 9, pp. 854-855.

TIETZE, Hans. "Wiens heiliger Frühling war Klimts Werk" *Kunstchronik,* XIX (1917-1918), 21.

VERGO. Peter. *Art in Vienna 1898-1918.* London: Phaidon, 1975.

VERGO, Peter. "Gustav Klimts Philosophie und das Programm der Universitätsgemälde" *Mitteilungen der Österreichischen Galerie,* XXII-XXIII (1978-1979), pp. 94-97.

WEIXLGÄRTNER, Alexander. "Gustav Klimt" *Die Graphischen Künste,* XXXV (1912), pp. 49-66.

WERNER, Alfred. *Gustav Klimt.* 100 drawings. New York: Dover, 1972.

ZUCKERKANDL, Bertha Szeps. "Der Klimt Fries" *Wiener Allgemeine Zeitung,* 10.23.1911, pp. 2-3.

ZUCKERKANDL, Bertha Szeps. "Eine reinliche Scheidung soll es sein", *Neues Wiener Journal,* 2.5.1931.

ZUCKERKANDL, Bertha Szeps. "Einiges über Klimt" *Volkszeitung,* 2.6.1936.

ILLUSTRATIONS